Building a Firm
Foundation

The Christian Foundation

THE CHRISTIAN FOUNDATION

Copyright © By Robert Crentsil On August 1, 2013
Second Edition – May 17 2021
Third Edition – December 2024
United States of America

All Rights Reserved: Printed in the United States of America. No part of this publication may be reproduced or transmitted in any form or means without written permission from the author.

All scripture quotations, unless otherwise indicated are taken from The King James Version of the Holy Bible.
Scripture Quotations Marked AMP Are Taken From
The Amplified Version of the Holy Bible
By The Lockman Foundation

Scripture Quotations Marked NIV Are Taken From
The New International Version of the Holy Bible:
Copyright © 1973, 1978, 1974 by International Bible Society
Used By Permission of Zondervan Publishing House
All Rights Reserved

Scripture Quotations Marked NASB Are Taken From
The New American Standard Bible of the Holy Bible
Copyright ©1960, 1962, 1963, 1968, 1971, 1972, 1973, 1975, 1977, 1995 by the Lockman Foundation

CONTACT INFORMATION:

E-Mail: apostlecrentsil1@gmail.com
Website: doxaglobalinc.org

DEDICATION & ACKNOWLDGMENT

THE CHRISTIAN FOUNDATION – This Book is dedicated to all who desire to be ALL that God intended and destined them to be, but due to a multiplicity of circumstances, find themselves overwhelmed by failure and defeat.

I dedicate this book to my wife: Rev. Mrs. Georgina Happy Crentsil. It is a great honor that you availed yourself for God, to use you to encourage me to finish this book. You are indeed a Woman of Valor. *"Favor is deceitful, and beauty is vain: but a woman that fears the Lord, she shall be praised"* Prov. 31:30

I dedicate this Book to my Sons: Samuel, Robert-Jesu, Prince-Charles and his wife Susan; To Nicholas, Joel-Kevin and my precious daughter: Princess-Olive Ewurabena Crentsil and Grandsons: Caleb-Joshua and Adin-Charles, Jude-Anthony, & David Sean. I pray that the Almighty God will watch over you and empower you to fully fulfill your God-given-potential and purpose and bring meaning, hope and joy to humanity.

I dedicate this Book to Dr. Jane Lowder – Director: CPT, Rev. Debbie Slayton, David Henderson and all leaders, Staff and Volunteers of Calvary Pentecostal Tabernacle, Ashland VA: Thank you for your great support. I am so appreciative of the hours of painstaking review and revision put into this document by Rev. Debbie Slayton, Barbara Buis, Carmen Warren, Patricia Holden, John D. Loewen, Glenn and Roseanne Leaflow, Patrick and Genevieve Tshiteya who helped in editing the Book.

To all Members, Partners and Supporters of Doxa Global Incorporated and the entire Body of Christ, I say thank you and God Bless You!

Above all, I dedicate this Book to You Holy Spirit for Your Presence, Illumination, Love and Refining Fire in my Life. To God be ALL the GLORY for entrusting me with this wonderful gift and the inspiration to express it in writing. Amen!

Apostle Dr. Robert Crentsil is the Founding President & Executive Director of Doxa Global Incorporated and Doxa Elite Bible College with the International Headquarters established in the United States of America.

Apostle Dr. Robert Crentsil is called to the Apostolic Prophetic Office. He is a Spiritual Father, an Author, a renowned Red Hot Bible Preacher/Teacher, Conference Speaker, Church Planter, and a man with a strong passion to see the birthing of a fresh Spiritual Revolution to impact and transform the Body of Christ & Humanity, The Greatest Harvest of Souls and Socio-Economic Transformation.

Apostle Dr. Robert Crentsil is the Author of "Turn The Battle To The Gate, Repoussez L'ennemi Jusqu'à Ses Portes; Spiritual Armament, The Christian Foundation, Positive Confession For Maximum Impact and Engaging God For His Manifested Presence.

THE CHRISTAIN FOUNDATION

Keys to Understanding, Recovering, Developing & Deploying Your God-Given Vision, Power, Authority & Dominion.
Keys to Revival, Reformation, Restoration, & Transformation.
Keys to Holy Spirit Empowerment & Biblical Revolution.
Keys To Divine Elevation & Alignment, Territorial Recovery, Dominance & Advancement.

"Then they that gladly received his word were baptized: and the same day there were added unto them about three thousand souls.

"And they continued steadfastly in the apostles' doctrine and fellowship, and in breaking of bread, and in prayers. And fear came upon every soul: and many wonders and signs were done by the apostles.

"And all that believed were together and had all things common; And sold their possessions and goods, and parted them to all men, as every man had need. And they, continuing daily with one accord in the temple, and breaking bread from house to house, did eat their meat with gladness and singleness of heart, Praising God, and having favor with all the people. And the Lord added to the church daily such as should be saved."

Saved & Translated

"For this cause we also, since the day we heard it, do not cease to pray for you, and to desire that ye might be filled with the knowledge of his will in all wisdom and spiritual understanding; That ye might walk worthy of the Lord unto all pleasing, being fruitful in every good work, and increasing in the knowledge of God; Strengthened with all might, according to his glorious power, unto all patience and longsuffering with joyfulness.

"Giving thanks unto the Father, which hath made us meet to be partakers of the inheritance of the saints in light: Who hath delivered us from the power of darkness, and hath translated us into the kingdom of his dear Son: In whom we have redemption through his blood, even the forgiveness of sins:

The Preeminence of Christ

"Who is the image of the invisible God, the firstborn of every creature: For by him were all things created, that are in heaven, and that are in earth, visible and invisible, whether they be thrones, or dominions, or principalities, or powers: all things were created by him, and for him: And he is before all things, and by him all things consist. And he is the head of the body, the church: who is the beginning, the firstborn from the dead; that in all things he might have the preeminence. Colossians 2:6-10

Saved By Grace Through Faith

Ephesians 2:1 - "And you hath he quickened, who were dead in trespasses and sins; Wherein in time past ye walked according to the course of this world, according to the prince of the power of the air, the spirit that now worketh in the children of disobedience: Among whom also we all had our conversation in times past in the lusts of our flesh, fulfilling the desires of the flesh and of the mind; and were by nature the children of wrath, even as others.

"But God, who is rich in mercy, for his great love wherewith he loved us, Even when we were dead in sins, hath quickened us together with Christ, (by grace ye are saved;) And hath raised us up together, and made us sit together in heavenly places in Christ Jesus. That in the ages to come he might shew the exceeding riches of his grace in his kindness toward us through Christ Jesus.

"For by grace are ye saved through faith; and that not of yourselves: it is the gift of God. Not of works, lest any man should boast. For we are his workmanship, created in Christ Jesus unto good works, which God hath before ordained that we should walk in them."

New Creation In Christ Jesus

II Corinthians 5:17-21 *"Therefore if any man be in Christ, he is a new creature: old things are passed away; behold, all things are become new. And all things are of God, who hath reconciled us to himself by Jesus Christ, and hath given to us the ministry of reconciliation; To wit, that God was in Christ, reconciling the world unto himself, not imputing their trespasses unto them; and hath committed unto us the word of reconciliation. Now then we are ambassadors for Christ, as though God did beseech you by us: we pray you in Christ's stead, be ye reconciled to God. For he hath made him to be sin for us, who knew no sin; that we might be made the righteousness of God in him."*

Colossians 2:6-10 "As ye have therefore received Christ Jesus the Lord, so walk ye in him: Rooted and built up in him, and stablished in the faith, as ye have been taught, abounding therein with thanksgiving. Beware lest any man spoil you through philosophy and vain deceit, after the tradition of men, after the rudiments of the world, and not after Christ. For in him dwelleth all the fulness of the Godhead bodily. And ye are complete in him, which is the head of all principality and power."

TABLE OF CONTENTS

Dedication

Chapter I Salvation & Assurance Of Salvation 11

Chapter II Water Baptism 33

Chapter III Holy Spirit Baptism 43

Chapter IV The Gifts of The Holy Spirit 69

Chapter V The Fruit Of The Recreated Spirit 81

Chapter VI Redemption, Deliverance, Healing, Restoration 97

Chapter VII Basic Doctrines Of The Bible 115

Chapter VIII Angels 123

Chapter IX 7 Dispensations: Seasons Of God's Dealings With Man ..157

Chapter X Principles Of Financial Stewardship 171

Salvation & Assurance Of Salvation

John 3:16-21 "For God so loved the world, that he gave his only begotten Son, that whosoever believeth in him should not perish, but have everlasting life. For God sent not his Son into the world to condemn the world; but that the world through him might be saved. He that believeth on him is not condemned: but he that believeth not is condemned already, because he hath not believed in the name of the only begotten Son of God. And this is the condemnation, that light is come into the world, and men loved darkness rather than light, because their deeds were evil. For everyone that doeth evil hateth the light, neither cometh to the light, lest his deeds should be reproved. But he that doeth truth cometh to the light, that his deeds may be made manifest, that they are wrought in God."

Lesson 1
Salvation & Assurance Of Salvation

Salvation is freedom from the curse of the law. Salvation is the forgiveness of sins through the Blood of Jesus Christ. It is total emancipation from Sin and the curse of sin, and iniquity, danger, spiritual conflict, sickness, diseases, troubled minds, hell, Satan, and witchcraft. The Greek word for salvation is sozo, which is also translated: "save," "heal," "make whole," or "deliver". In the Bible, sozo is used to convey a broader meaning than just being saved or forgiven of sins. It can also mean being physically healed of diseases or being delivered from an enemy, such as the devil and his demons.

Another Greek word related to salvation is soteria, which means "rescue" or "deliverance from danger, destruction, and peril". The word soteria comes from the word soter, which means "savior". The branch of theology that studies salvation is called soteriology, which also comes from the Greek word soterion meaning "salvation".

The Fall Of Man – (Genesis 3 Account)

God created Man in His image after His Likeness. Male and Female, God Created them. Man was created as a free moral agent. God gave man the free will to worship and serve Him. The relationship between God and Man was cordial, consistent and strong in the Garden of Eden. Adam and Eve were God's handiwork, the epitome of His creation. Man was set apart by God Jehovah to represent and manifest HIM – demonstrate His Glory in every sphere of life. God MADE Adam and Eve to be administrators and caretakers of His Creation.

Lucifer (Satan) entered (Possessed) the Serpent and deceived Adam and Eve to disobey God by eating the forbidden fruit. They sinned against God's Word and tried to cover-up by hiding themselves with leaves. Sin separated Adam and Eve from God's presence.

Adam, Eve, and the Serpent were cursed by God. Adam and Eve were driven out of the Garden of Eden. So he drove out the man; and he placed at the east of the garden of Eden Cherubims, and a flaming sword which turned every way, to keep the way of the tree of life and affliction witnessed in all generations.

This Curse and Sin nature consequently fell on all humanity by inheritance. Adam and Eve lost the dominion, authority and moral responsibility God invested in the. Lucifer and his fallen angels became the new Landlords of Planet Earth.

The Fall of Man - Genesis 3:1-24 (The Amplified Bible)

"Now the serpent was more crafty (subtle, skilled in deceit) than any living creature of the field which the Lord God had made. And [a] the serpent (Satan) said to the woman, "Can it really be that God has said, 'You shall not eat from [b] any tree of the garden'?" [2] And the woman said to the serpent, "We may eat fruit from the trees of the garden, [3] except the fruit from the tree which is in the middle of the garden. God said, 'You shall not eat from it nor touch it, otherwise you will die.'" [4] But the serpent said to the woman, "You certainly will not die! [5] For God knows that on the day you eat from it your eyes will be opened [that is, you will have greater awareness], and you will be like God, knowing [the difference between] good and evil." [6] And when the woman saw that the tree was good for food, and that it was delightful to look at, and a tree to be desired in order to make one wise and insightful, she took some of its fruit and ate it; and she also gave some to her husband [c] with her,

Biblical Foundation For Spiritual Growth & Maturity

and he ate. ⁷ Then the eyes of the two of them were opened [that is, their awareness increased], and they knew that they were naked; and they fastened fig leaves together and made themselves coverings. And they heard the sound of the Lord God walking in the garden in the cool [afternoon breeze] of the day, so the man and his wife hid and kept themselves hidden from the [d]presence of the Lord God among the trees of the garden. ⁹ But the Lord God called to Adam, and said to him, "Where are you?" ¹⁰ He said, I heard the sound of You [walking] in the garden, and I was afraid because I was naked; so I hid myself." ¹¹ God said, "Who told you that you were naked? Have you eaten [fruit] from the tree of which I commanded you not to eat?" ¹² And the man said, "The woman whom You gave to be with me—she gave me [fruit] from the tree, and I ate it." ¹³ Then the Lord God said to the woman, "What is this that you have done?" And the woman said, "The serpent beguiled and deceived me, and I ate [from the forbidden tree]."

¹⁴ The Lord God said to the serpent, "Because you have done this, You are cursed more than all the cattle, And more than any animal of the field; On your belly you shall go, And dust you shall eat All the days of your life. ¹⁵ "And I will put enmity (open hostility) Between you and the woman, And between your seed (offspring) and her [e]Seed; He shall [fatally] bruise your head, And you shall [only] bruise His heel."

¹⁶ To the woman He said, "I will greatly multiply Your pain in childbirth; In pain you will give birth to children; Yet your desire and longing will be for your husband, And he will rule [with authority] over you and be responsible for you. Then to Adam the Lord God said, "Because you have listened [attentively] to the voice of your wife, and have eaten [fruit] from the tree about which I commanded you, saying, 'You shall not eat of it; The ground is [now] under a curse because of you; In sorrow and toil you shall eat [the fruit] of it, All the days of your life. ¹⁸ "Both thorns and thistles it shall grow for you; And you shall eat the plants of the field ¹⁹

"By the sweat of your face You will eat bread Until you return to the ground, For from it you were taken; For you are dust, And to dust you shall return."

[20] *The man named his wife Eve (life spring, life giver), because she was the mother of all the living.* [21] *The Lord God made tunics of [animal] skins for Adam and his wife and clothed them.* [22] *And the Lord God said, "Behold, the man has become like one of Us (Father, Son, Holy Spirit), knowing [how to distinguish between] good and evil; and now, he might stretch out his hand, and take from the tree of life as well, and eat [its fruit], and live [in this fallen, sinful condition] forever"—* [23] *therefore the Lord God sent Adam away from the Garden of Eden, to till and cultivate the ground from which he was taken.* [24] *So God drove the man out; and at the east of the Garden of Eden He [permanently] stationed the [l]cherubim and the sword with the flashing blade which turned round and round [in every direction] to protect and guard the way (entrance, access) to the tree of life."*

Understanding Ezekiel's Prophecy On Salvation

Ezekiel 36:25-30 *"Then will I sprinkle clean water upon you, and ye shall be clean: from all your filthiness, and from all your idols, will I cleanse you. A new heart also will I give you, and a new spirit will I put within you: and I will take away the stony heart out of your flesh, and I will give you an heart of flesh. And I will put my spirit within you, and cause you to walk in my statutes, and ye shall keep my judgments, and do them. And ye shall dwell in the land that I gave to your fathers; and ye shall be my people, and I will be your God. I will also save you from all your uncleanness: and I will call for the corn, and will increase it, and lay no famine upon you. And I will multiply the fruit of the tree, and the increase of the field, that ye shall receive no more reproach of famine among the heathen."*

Biblical Foundation For Spiritual Growth & Maturity

Exposition On Ezekiel 36:25-30

v. 25a *"Then will I sprinkle clean water upon you"* Clean water is the cleansing power of God's Word. Symbolically, water used outwardly, stands for the cleansing power of God's Word. Water used internally stands for the life-giving power of the Holy Spirit. This context speaks of the power of God's word to deliver, heal, cleanse, and give life to the sinner from spiritual death, bondage, and enslavement. *John 3:5 "Jesus answered, verily, verily I say unto thee: except a man be born of water and of the Spirit, he cannot enter into the kingdom of God. John 15:3 "Now ye are clean through the word which I have spoken unto you."*

v. 26 "A new heart also will I give you, and a new spirit will I put within you: and I will take away the stony heart out of your flesh, and I will give you an heart of flesh." – This Means "Recreation of the Human Spirit" Or To "Be Born Again" John 3:5; I Corinthians 5:17-21

v. 27a "I Will Put My Spirit Within You" – This refers to the Holy Spirit indwelling the new Christian at Salvation. The purpose of the indwelling Holy Spirit is to Quicken, Save, give Everlasting Life, Spiritual and Physical Empowerment

v. 27b "and cause you to walk in my statutes, and ye shall keep my judgments, and do them." This is to enable the Believer to walk in Obedience to God's Statutes, Ordinances, and Live a Transformed life
1. Keep God's judgments and do them
2. Abide in Christ Jesus
3. Walk in obedience to God's Word and Bear Fruit

v. 28a "And ye shall dwell in the land that I gave to your fathers"- The Believer's Possession; Spiritual Inheritance and Physical Prosperity – Romans 8; Colossians 1:12-14; I Corinthians 2:1-16

v. 28b "Ye Shall Be My People, And I Will Be Your God – Ephesians 1,2; John 1:11,12; I Corinthians 1, 2, 3, 6; Galatians; II Corinthians 5:17-21

v. 29 "I Will Also Save You From All Uncleanness: Cleansing of all sins and iniquity through the Blood of Jesus. *I John 1:8-10 "If we say that we have no sin, we deceive ourselves, and the truth is not in us. If we confess our sins, he is faithful and just to forgive us our sins, and to cleanse us from all unrighteousness."*

v. 30 The Promise Of Prosperity For The Believer: "…*and I will call for the corn, and will increase it, and lay no famine upon you. And I will multiply the fruit of the tree, and the increase of the field, that ye shall receive no more reproach of famine among the heathen."*

FULFILLMENT Of Ezekiel 36 Prophecy – John 3

Salvation Is God's Gift To Humanity. Repent, Believe & Accept The Lord Jesus Christ Into Your Heart. Confess (Profess) Him As Your Savior & Lord. *Jesus answered and said unto him, Verily, verily, I say unto thee: Except a man be born again, he cannot see the kingdom of God. Nicodemus saith unto him: How can a man be born when he is old? can he enter the second time into his mother's womb, and be born? Jesus answered, Verily, verily, I say unto thee: Except a man be born of water and of the Spirit, he cannot enter into the kingdom of God. That which is born of the flesh is flesh; and that which is born of the Spirit* is spirit. Marvel not that I said unto thee, Ye must be born again. The wind bloweth where it listeth, and thou hearest the sound thereof, but canst not tell whence it cometh, and whither it goeth: so is every one that is born of the Spirit. Nicodemus answered and said unto him: How can these things be? Jesus answered and said unto him, Art thou a master of Israel, and knowest not these things?

"Verily, verily, I say unto thee: We speak that we do know and testify that we have seen; and ye receive not our witness. If I have told you earthly things, and ye believe not, how shall ye believe, if I tell you of heavenly things? And no man hath ascended up to heaven, but he that came down from heaven, even the Son of man which is in heaven. And as Moses lifted up the serpent in the wilderness, even so must the Son of man be lifted up: That whosoever believeth in him should not perish, but have eternal life.

"For God so loved the world, that he gave his only begotten Son, that whosoever believeth in him should not perish, but have everlasting life. For God sent not his Son into the world to condemn the world; but that the world through him might be saved. He that believeth on him is not condemned: but he that believeth not is condemned already, because he hath not believed in the name of the only begotten Son of God.

"And this is the condemnation, that light is come into the world, and men loved darkness rather than light, because their deeds were evil. For everyone that doeth evil hateth the light, neither cometh to the light, lest his deeds should be reproved. But he that doeth truth cometh to the light, that his deeds may be made manifest, that they are wrought in God."

The Christian Foundation

Steps To Salvation

1. Repent – Acts 2:35-39 *"Now when they heard this, they were pricked in their heart, and said unto Peter and to the rest of the apostles, Men and brethren, what shall we do? Then Peter said unto them, Repent, and be baptized every one of you in the name of Jesus Christ for the remission of sins, and ye shall receive the gift of the Holy Ghost. For the promise is unto you, and to your children, and to all that are afar off, even as many as the Lord our God shall call."*

2. Accept - Accept that you are a sinner and that you cannot save yourself. *Romans 3:23 "For all have sinned and come short of the glory of God."*
- *Romans 6:23 "For the wages of sin is death but the gift of God is eternal life through Jesus Christ our Lord.*
- *Romans 5:8 'But God commendeth His Love toward us in that, while we were yet sinners, Christ died for us.*

3. Believe In Christ Jesus - Believe that Christ Jesus came to die for your sins, to redeem/buy you out of bondage (Out of Satan's Slave Market) with His own Blood from the curse of sin and iniquity. Repent of your sin.

John 3:16,17 "For God so loved the world, that he gave his only begotten Son, that whosoever believeth in him should not perish, but have everlasting life. For God sent not his Son into the world to condemn the world; but that the world through him might be saved."

Romans 10:8b-13 The word is nigh thee, even in thy mouth, and in thy heart: that is, the word of faith, which we preach; That if thou shalt confess with thy mouth the Lord Jesus, and shalt believe in thine heart that God hath raised him from the dead, thou shalt be saved.

"For with the heart man believeth unto righteousness; and with the mouth confession is made unto salvation. For the scripture saith: Whosoever believeth on him shall not be ashamed. For there is no difference between the Jew and the Greek: for the same Lord over all is rich unto all that call upon him. For whosoever shall call upon the name of the Lord shall be saved."

4. Confession Of Sin - Confess Your Sins: Past, Present - Confession Of Sin Leads To Mercy, Grace, Forgiveness And Peace - *I John 1:8-10 "If we say that we have no sin, we deceive ourselves, and the truth is not in us. If we confess our sins, he is faithful and just to forgive us our sins, and to cleanse us from all unrighteousness."*

5. Declare Jesus Christ As Your Lord And Saviour - Receive Jesus Christ into your heart as your Lord and Savior. Accepting Jesus into your heart results in restoration of fellowship with the Father and imputation of righteousness, life, power, and authority - the right, privilege to be God's Rev. 3:20; John 1:11, 12

Hebrews 10:19-25 *"Having therefore, brethren, boldness to enter into the holiest by the blood of Jesus, By a new and living way, which he hath consecrated for us, through the veil, that is to say, his flesh; And having an high priest over the house of God;*

"Let us draw near with a true heart in full assurance of faith, having our hearts sprinkled from an evil conscience, and our bodies washed with pure water.

"Let us hold fast the profession of our faith without wavering; (for he is faithful that promised;)"

Pray The Prayer Of Salvation

Father, I thank you for this timely opportunity given me to put my life back on track.

I know I am a sinner.

I cannot save myself.

I thank you for sending Jesus Christ to die on the cross for my sins.

I acknowledge my sins before you today and ask for your forgiveness.

Father forgive me and cleanse me with your blood and save me.

Lord Jesus, I confess you today as my Savior and accept you as my Lord.

Lord Jesus, come into my HEART today and make me a new person.

Father I thank you for hearing my prayer and saving me in the name of Jesus.

Amen!

Thank You Father For Saving Me Today!

I Am Saved!!!

Assurance Of Salvation (Your Position In Christ)

Assurance of Salvation - This Confirms & Affirms What Happens as a result of Believing and Accepting Christ Jesus As Personal Lord & Savior

1. You Are Reconnected To God's Plan And Purpose
Ephesians 1:3-6 "Blessed be the God and Father of our Lord Jesus Christ, who hath blessed us with all spiritual blessings in heavenly places in Christ: According as he hath chosen us in him before the foundation of the world, that we should be holy and without blame before him in love: Having predestinated us unto the adoption of children by Jesus Christ to himself, according to the good pleasure of his will, To the praise of the glory of his grace, wherein he hath made us accepted in the beloved."

2. You Are Saved By Grace, Resurrected From Spiritual Death (Separation From The Father).
Ephesians 2:1-10 "And you hath he quickened, who were dead in trespasses and sins; Wherein in time past ye walked according to the course of this world, according to the prince of the power of the air, the spirit that now worketh in the children of disobedience: Among whom also we all had our conversation in times past in the lusts of our flesh, fulfilling the desires of the flesh and of the mind; and were by nature the children of wrath, even as others. But God, who is rich in mercy, for his great love wherewith he loved us: Even when we were dead in sins, hath quickened us together with Christ, (by grace ye are saved;) And hath raised us up together and made us sit together in heavenly places in Christ Jesus: That in the ages to come he might shew the exceeding riches of his grace in his kindness toward us through Christ Jesus.

THE CHRISTIAN FOUNDATION

"For by grace are ye saved through faith; and that not of yourselves: it is the gift of God: Not of works, lest any man should boast. For we are his workmanship, created in Christ Jesus unto good works, which God hath before ordained that we should walk in them."

3. You Are Saved If You Have Accepted Jesus As Your Lord & Savior - *John 3:16-18 "For God so loved the world that he gave his only begotten Son, that whosoever believeth in him should not perish, but have everlasting life. For God sent not his Son into the world to condemn the world; but that the world through him might be saved. He that believeth on him is not condemned: but he that believeth not is condemned already, because he hath not believed in the name of the only begotten Son of God. And this is the condemnation, that light is come into the world, and men loved darkness rather than light, because their deeds were evil. For everyone that doeth evil hateth the light, neither cometh to the light, lest his deeds should be reproved. But he that doeth truth cometh to the light that his deeds may be made manifest, that they are wrought in God."*

4. Jesus Takes Residence In The Heart Of The New Christian *Revelation 3:20 "Behold, I stand at the door, and knock: if any man hears my voice, and open the door, I will come in to him, and will sup with him, and he with me."*

5. Washed In The Blood Of Jesus. Delivered From The Kingdom Of Darkness And Translated Into The Kingdom Of His Dear Son. You Are Given An Inheritance – *Colossians 1:12 -14 "Giving thanks unto the Father, which hath made us meet to be partakers of the inheritance of the saints in light: Who hath delivered us from the power of* *darkness, and hath translated us into the kingdom of his dear Son: In whom we have redemption through his blood, even the forgiveness of sins:"*

6. All Curses Of Life (Past, Present & Future) Are Nailed To the Cross Of Christ Jesus - *Galatians 3:13,14 "Christ hath redeemed us from the curse of the law, being made a curse for us: for it is written, Cursed is every one that hangeth on a tree: That the blessing of Abraham might come on the Gentiles through Jesus Christ; that we might receive the promise of the Spirit through faith."*

7. You Are Made A New Creation - *II Corinthians 5:17-21 "Therefore, if any man be in Christ, he is a new creature: old things are passed away; behold all things are become new. And all things are of God, who hath reconciled us to himself by Jesus Christ, and hath given to us the ministry of reconciliation. To wit, that God was in Christ, reconciling the world unto himself, not imputing their trespasses unto them; and hath committed unto us the word of reconciliation.*

8. You Are An Ambassador For Christ Jesus *II Cor. 5:20 "Now then we are ambassadors for Christ, as though God did beseech you by us: we pray you in Christ's stead, be ye reconciled to God. For He hath made him to be sin for us, who knew no sin; that we might be made the righteousness of God in him."*

9. You Are Made Righteous In Christ Jesus - *II Corinthians 5:21 "For he hath made him to be sin for us, who knew no sin; that we might be made the righteousness of God in him."*

10. Given AUTHORITY (GK. EXOUSIA). The Right And Privilege To Be God's Child - *John 1:11,12 "He came unto his own, and his own received him not. But as many as received him, to them gave He power to become the sons of God, even to them that believe on his name"*

11. Eternally Sealed You With The Holy Ghost - *Ephesians 1:13,14 "In whom ye also trusted, after that ye heard the word of truth, the gospel of your salvation: in whom also after that ye believed, ye were sealed with that holy Spirit of promise: Which is the earnest of our inheritance until the redemption of the purchased possession, unto the praise of his glory."*

12. Seated In Heavenly Places With Christ Jesus *Ephesians 2:5,6 "Even when we were dead in sins, hath quickened us together with Christ, (by grace ye are saved;) And hath raised us up together, and made us sit together in heavenly places in Christ Jesus"*

13. Made Priest and King To Reign On Earth - *Revelation1:5,6; 5:10 "Unto him that loved us, and washed us from our sins in his own blood: And hath made us kings and priests unto God and his Father; to him be glory and dominion for ever and ever." Amen.*

14. You Are The Workmanship Of Christ - Ephesians *2:10 "For we are his workmanship, created in Christ Jesus unto good works, which God hath before ordained that we should walk in them."*

15. You Are Complete In Christ. You Blessed With The Blessings Of Abraham. You Are The Reflection Of God's Glory

Colossians 2:9,10; "For in him dwelleth all the fullness of the Godhead bodily. And ye are complete in him, which is the head of all principality and power"

Galatians 3:6-9 "Even as Abraham believed God, and it was accounted to him for righteousness. Know ye therefore that they which are of faith, the same are the children of Abraham.

"And the scripture, foreseeing that God would justify the heathen through faith, preached before the gospel unto Abraham, saying, In thee shall all nations be blessed. So then they which be of faith are blessed with faithful Abraham."

16. Power Of Attorney To The Name "JESUS" - *Philippians 2:4-12 and Mark 16:15-20 - "He that believeth and is baptized shall be saved; but he that believeth not shall be damned. And these signs shall follow them that believe.*

"In my name shall they cast out devils; they shall speak with new tongues; They shall take up serpents; and if they drink any deadly thing, it shall not hurt them; they shall lay hands on the sick, and they shall recover."

17. Keys To The Kingdom Of Heaven – *Matthew 16:17-19 "And Jesus answered and said unto him, Blessed art thou, Simon Barjona: for flesh and blood hath not revealed it unto thee, but my Father which is in heaven.*

"And I say also unto thee, That thou art Peter, and upon this rock I will build my church; and the gates of hell shall not prevail against it.

"And I will give unto thee the keys of the kingdom of heaven: and whatsoever thou shalt bind on earth shall be bound in heaven: and whatsoever thou shalt loose on earth shall be loosed in heaven."

Study Lesson I
Salvation

Define The Following

1. Perish _____

2. Condemn _____

3. Everlasting life _____

4. In your own words, expound on John 3:16-20 _____
_____

Cornelius - Acts 10

1. Cornelius is described as:

   a) _____

   b) _____

   c) _____

2. Cornelius had a vision. What did the angel of the Lord tell him to do? _____
_____
_____
_____

3. Did Cornelius do as he was told? _____

Apostle Peter (Acts 10)

1. What was Peter's other name? _____

2. Peter had a vision. Describe what he was told
_____
_____

3. How many times was he told? _____

4. While Peter was thinking about the vision, what did the Spirit of the Lord tell him?
_____
_____

5. Briefly describe the message that Peter had for Cornelius and his people?
_____
_____
_____

6. When Peter was delivering his message, what happened to the People at Cornelius house?
_____
_____
_____

Define The Following:

Biblical Foundation For Spiritual Growth & Maturity

1. Born Again _____

2. The Kingdom of God? _____

3. In one word, what is the only way that we can enter the Kingdom of God?
_____

4. In your own words, what was the greatest thing that God did to show His love for us?
_____
_____

4. Complete this sentence: Jesus is the _____ of the world.

6. Alms means _____
_____
_____

8. What are the Benefits of Salvation? _____
_____
_____

9. How Do You Win Someone to Christ? _____

Steps To Salvation

THE CHRISTIAN FOUNDATION

What are the four steps to salvation as stated on pages 11 and 12? Briefly explain each step.

1. _____

2. _____

3. _____

4. _____

5. _____

Review Questions

1. What Is Salvation? _____

_____

_____

2. Jesus said a man must be born of two things. One was explained to Nicodemus and the other explained to Cornelius.
a) Which one was explained to Nicodemus and how was it explained?
_____

_____

b) Which one was explained to Cornelius and how was it explained?
_____

3. Explain The Steps To Salvation.

Biblical Foundation For Spiritual Growth & Maturity

a) _____

b) _____

c) _____

d) _____

4. In John 3:5, what did Jesus mean when He said, "Except a man be born of water and of the Spirit"?

_____

Challenge Question

1. How Does The Vision Peter Had in Acts 10 Relates To Salvation? _____

_____

2. Summarize the events that took place from the time that Cornelius had a vision until the people received the Baptism of the Holy Ghost. (Use Additional Sheets)

3. What impact does this chapter have on the ministry for which God has called us today? (Use Additional Sheets)

Water Baptism

Romans 6:3-9 "Know ye not, that so many of us as were baptized into Jesus Christ were baptized into his death? Therefore, we are buried with him by baptism into death: that like as Christ was raised up from the dead by the glory of the Father, even so we also should walk in newness of life. For if we have been planted together in the likeness of his death, we shall be also in the likeness of his resurrection: Knowing this, that our old man is crucified with him, that the body of sin might be destroyed, that henceforth we should not serve sin. For he that is dead is freed from sin. Now if we be dead with Christ, we believe that we shall also live with him: Knowing that Christ being raised from the dead dieth no more; death hath no more dominion over him."

Lesson 2
Water Baptism

And he said unto them, Go ye into all the world and preach the gospel to every creature. He that believeth and is baptized shall be saved; but he that believeth not shall be damned. And these signs shall follow them that believe. In my name shall they cast out devils; they shall speak with new tongues; They shall take up serpents; and if they drink any deadly thing, it shall not hurt them; they shall lay hands on the sick, and they shall recover." Amen!" Mark 16:15-20

Matthew 3:11, 12 "I indeed baptize you with water unto repentance. but he that cometh after me is mightier than I, whose shoes I am not worthy to bear, he shall baptize you with the Holy Ghost, and with fire: Whose fan is in his hand, and he will throughly purge his floor, and gather his wheat into the garner; but he will burn up the chaff with unquenchable fire."

Acts 2:38-41 "Now when they heard this, they were pricked in their heart, and said unto Peter and to the rest of the apostles, Men and brethren, what shall we do?

" Then Peter said unto them, Repent, and be baptized every one of you in the name of Jesus Christ for the remission of sins, and ye shall receive the gift of the Holy Ghost.

Rom. 6 "Know ye not, that so many of us as were baptized into Jesus Christ were baptized into his death? Therefore, we are buried with him by baptism into death: that like as Christ was raised up from the dead by the glory of the Father, even so we also should walk in newness of life."

Understanding Water Baptism

Water Baptism is an outward sign of an inward change. The word "Baptism" comes from the Greek word "baptizo," which means "To Immerse." Water Baptism is done by immersing the Believer into water, identifying with the Death, Burial and the Resurrection of Jesus Christ. Water Baptism does not guarantee salvation. It is our faith in Christ Jesus that results in Salvation. Obedience in Water Baptism fulfills righteousness.

Water Baptism is for those who have received Jesus Christ as Lord and Savior and have reached the age of accountability. Infants are not to be Baptized. This is because they have no control over the knowledge of good and evil and must be dedicated to the Lord.

The candidate for Water Baptism must understand the Gospel message of salvation; convicted of his sins and repented; understand and identify with the death, burial, and the resurrection of Jesus Christ and finally has accepted Christ Jesus as Personal Lord and Savior.

Whether one is baptized in the "Name of Jesus" or "The Father, Son, and the Holy Ghost (Spirit)" it is all done with one meaning: "Death, Burial, and Resurrection of Jesus Christ, to walk in a newness of life." It is still the outward sign of an inward change. God is One, not three.

The Great Commission in Matthew instructs us to Baptize the Believer in the name of the Father, Son, and the holy Spirit. Mark's Gospel instructs us to Baptize in the Name of Jesus. In the Book of Acts, the Apostles Baptized in the name of Jesus.

Biblical Foundation For Spiritual Growth & Maturity

Where there is no water, pool of water, river, sea, etc. any method can be used, and will be accepted by the Lord provided it does not violate Biblical Ethics and Doctrine or the Candidate's Rights in Life and Faith in Christ. The thief on the cross did not have the opportunity of getting baptized in water yet his repentant heart secured him a place in Christ's kingdom. Water Baptism does not make one a Christian; it is faith in Christ Jesus. Water Baptism is an outward sign of an inward change. – Matthew 28:18-20; Mark 16:15-20, Ephesians 4.

Ephesians 2:1-10 "And you hath he quickened, who were dead in trespasses and sins; Wherein in time past ye walked according to the course of this world, according to the prince of the power of the air, the spirit that now worketh in the children of disobedience: Among whom also we all had our conversation in times past in the lusts of our flesh, fulfilling the desires of the flesh and of the mind; and were by nature the children of wrath, even as others.

"But God, who is rich in mercy, for his great love wherewith he loved us, Even when we were dead in sins, hath quickened us together with Christ, (by grace ye are saved;) And hath raised us up together, and made us sit together in heavenly places in Christ Jesus: That in the ages to come he might shew the exceeding riches of his grace in his kindness toward us through Christ Jesus.

"For By Grace Are Ye Saved Through Faith; And That Not Of Yourselves: It Is The Gift Of God: Not Of Works, Lest Any Man Should Boast. For We Are His Workmanship, Created In Christ Jesus Unto Good Works, Which God Hath Before Ordained That We Should Walk In Them.

The Three Baptisms For The Believer
1. **Baptism Into The Body Of Christ** - Normally referred to as "One Baptism." At salvation, the new Christian is "birthed into" or "received into" the Body of Christ. This is a spiritual experience. This is conducted by the Holy Spirit - Ephesians 4:4-6

2. **Baptism In Water By Immersion** – This is a Physical experience of immersing a new Believer into water; identifying with the death, burial, and the resurrection of Jesus. Mk 16:15-20; Rom. 6:3-5

3. **Baptism In The Holy Spirit** - This is the empowerment of the Holy Spirit (infusion of God's supernatural ability) in the life of the believer for Worship and Service. By this Baptism, the Holy Spirit empowers the believer to become an ardent witness for Jesus Christ. Jesus is the sole baptizer of the Holy Spirit. Matt. 3:11, 12; Luke 24:49 and Acts 1:8. The initial evidence of this Baptism is speaking in an unknown tongue. Joel 2:28, 29; Lk 24:49; Acts 2:1-5, 8.

Examples Of Water Baptism
1. John the Baptist by river Jordan & Aenon Matthew 3:1-10; John 3:23
2. John the Baptist Baptizes Jesus Christ by Immersion Matthew 3:13-17
3. Water Baptism in the Early Church - Acts 3:37-47
4. Phillip Baptizes the Ethiopian Eunuch - Acts 8:12-40
5. Cornelius and his household Baptized - Acts 10:44-48
6. Lydia Baptized by Apostle Paul - Acts 16:13-15
7. Believers in Ephesus Baptized - Acts 19:1-7

Study Lesson II
Water Baptism

Define The Following

1. Repentance _____

2. Baptism _____

3. Remission _____

Key Character References

Father

Who is the Father? _____

List two qualities of the Father?

_____

Son

Who is the Son? _____

List two qualities of the Son?

a)_____

b)_____

Holy Ghost

Who is the Holy Ghost? _____

List two qualities of the Holy Ghost? ____

_____

The Christian Foundation

Key Scriptural References

Matthew 28:18-20

Jesus instructs the disciples first to
_____ and

then to _____ and finally _____ in

the name of the _____ the _____ and

the _____

What must the nations be taught? _____

_____

_____

Mark 16:15-20

To whom did Jesus commission His disciples to preach?

_____

_____

List the signs that must follow every believer:

a) _____

b) _____

c) _____

d) _____

Biblical Foundation For Spiritual Growth & Maturity

Three Baptisms for the Believer

1. What are the three baptisms for the believer? Explain each.

a)_____

b)_____

c)_____

2. List at least three examples of water baptism in this lesson?

a)_____

b)_____

c)_____

Review Questions

1. What is baptism? _____

_____

Why Baptism by immersion? _____

_____

2. Name the three baptisms and explain each (Include Scriptural References)

a)_____

b)_____

THE CHRISTIAN FOUNDATION

c) _____

3. Explain what is meant by baptism as an outward sign of an inward change? -Add References

4. Can a person be saved if he/she is not baptized? _____

If, yes, why is baptism necessary? _____

If no, what does baptism do to save a person? _____

Biblical Foundation For Spiritual Growth & Maturity

Challenge Questions

Explain, in detail: Mark 16:18a. Explain in detail: Matthew 3:11. Be sure to address the following:

1. What is the definition of "Baptism"?

2. What is baptism with water unto repentance

3. What is "Baptize you with fire and the Holy Ghost"

4. Explain Matthew 3:12; relate it to this present day.

5. Does water baptism lead to Salvation?

6. Matthew 28:19 speaks of baptism in the name of the Father, Son and the Holy Ghost, explain.

7. In whose name or what name are we to Baptize?

8. Why did the early Apostles baptize in the name of Jesus?

9. What is the difference between the name of "the name of Jesus" and "the name of the Father, Son and the Holy Ghost?

Baptism Of the Holy Spirit

"And when the day of Pentecost was fully come, they were all with one accord in one place. And suddenly there came a sound from heaven as of a rushing mighty wind, and it filled all the house where they were sitting. And there appeared unto them cloven tongues like as of fire, and it sat upon each of them. And they were all filled with the Holy Ghost, and began to speak with other tongues, as the Spirit gave them utterance. "Acts 2:1-4

Chapter 3
Baptism Of the Holy Spirit

The Holy Spirit is the "Third Person" of the Triune God. God is "One." He manifests Himself in three ways or Personalities. God Jehovah Elohim reveals Himself as: God the Father, God the Son (God's Word Incarnate, Jesus Christ), and God the Holy Spirit (The Spirit of the LORD GOD JEHOVAH). The Holy Spirit is God. As God Revealing Himself to Humanity from Creation, we are in the dispensation of "God the Holy Spirit." In the first Dispensation of God Revealing Himself, He made Himself known as Jehovah Elohim. In the New Testament, He revealed Himself as Jesus Christ. Jesus walked on Earth as the Express Image or Manifested Presence of Jehovah Elohim, and as God's Word Incarnate (Becoming Flesh and Dwelling Among Us). References: Genesis 1:1-3; John 1:1-5, 14; I Timothy 3:16; Hebrews 1:1-14; John 14:1-14

The Holy Spirit Is Revealed:

1. **In Genesis 1:2 As The Spirit Of God: -** *"And the earth was without form, and void; and darkness was upon the face of the deep. And the Spirit of God moved upon the face of the waters."*

2. **In Revelation 4:5-6 As Seven-Fold Holy Spirit -** *"And out of the throne proceeded lightnings and thunderings and voices: and there were seven* **lamps of fire burning before the throne, which are the seven Spirits of God.** *And before the throne there was a sea of glass like unto crystal: and in the midst of the throne, and round about the throne, were four beasts full of eyes before and behind."*

3. **In Isaiah 11:2 The Holy Spirit** is: *The spirit of the LORD; The spirit of wisdom; The spirit of understanding; The spirit of counsel; The spirit of might; the spirit of knowledge; The spirit of the fear of the LORD."*

4. **In John 14:15-21 As The Comforter -** *"If ye love me, keep my commandments. And I will pray the Father, and he shall give you another Comforter, that he may abide with you forever: Even the Spirit of truth; whom the world cannot receive because it seeth him not, neither knoweth him: but ye know him; for he dwelleth with you and shall be in you. I will not leave you comfortless: I will come to you."*

Symbols & Manifestations Of The Holy Spirit
(Few Of The Many Symbols Of The Holy Spirit)
- Dove - Peace, Wisdom,
- River - Life Giving, Restoration, Regeneration
- Water - Cleansing Power, God's Word, Guidance
- Light - Illumination, Direction, Instruction,
- Wine - Resilience, Zeal, Energy, Empowerment
- Seal - Completeness, Sanctioning - Done Deal
- Eagle - Strength, Fortitude, Foresight, Precision, Longsuffering, Stability
- Fire - Purification, Renewal, Restoration
- Cloud - Hope, Impending Glory, God's Glory
- Rain - New Beginnings - Revival, Restoration
- Wind - Favor, Cleansing Power, Restoration
- Compounded Oil or Butter – Anointing, Consecration, Sanctification, Dedication
- He Manifest Himself as: Widom, Revelation Knowledge, Understanding, Might, Resurrection Power etc.

The Holy Spirit In The Old Testament

At Genesis One Creation (Genesis 1:2) **The Holy Spirit Hoovered Over The Face Of The Waters -** The Holy Spirit is referred to as *"The Spirit of God." W*e see Him "Brooding or Hovering over" the chaotic state of the universe and giving creative and resurrection power to God's word to create. *Genesis 1:1-3 (The Amplified Bible) "In the beginning God (prepared, formed, fashioned, and) created the heavens and the earth. The earth was without form and an empty waste and darkness was upon the face of the very great deep. The Spirit of God was moving (hovering, brooding) over the face of the waters, and God said: Let there be light; and there was light."*

Old Testament Were Saints Empowered For A Season. They Were Not Filled Permanently – The Holy Spirit is God. Though very active from Pre-Adamite Age through creation and through the Old Testament, the Holy Spirit did not permanently abide in the hearts of Old Testament Saints. He "Came Upon" "Brooded Upon" "Empowered" them at each given moment (time) to accomplish a specific purpose and then left. The gifts of the Holy Spirit manifested momentarily.

For Example:

1. The Holy Spirit Upon Moses And The Seventy Elders

Numbers 11:16-17; 24-29; 24:2-3 (Amplified Bible) "And the Lord said to Moses, Gather for Me seventy men of the elders of Israel whom you know to be the elders of the people and officers over them; and bring them to the Tent of meeting and let them stand there with you.

"And I will come down and talk with you there; and I will take of the Spirit which is upon you and will put It upon them; and they shall bear the burden of the people with you, so that you may not have to bear it yourself alone. So Moses went out and told the people the words of the Lord, and he gathered seventy men of the elders of the people and set them round about the Tent.

"And the Lord came down in the cloud and spoke to him and took of the Spirit that was upon him and put it upon the seventy elders; and when the Spirit rested upon them, they prophesied [sounding forth the praises of God and declaring His will]. Then they did so no more.

"But there remained two men in the camp named Eldad and Medad. The Spirit rested upon them, and they were of those who were selected and listed, yet they did not go out to the Tent [as told to do], but they prophesied in the camp. And a young man ran to Moses and said: Eldad and Medad are prophesying [sounding forth the praises of God and declaring His will] in the camp.

"Joshua, son of Nun, the minister of Moses, one of his chosen men, said: My lord Moses, forbid them! But Moses said to him, Are you envious or jealous for my sake? Would that all the Lord's people were prophets and that the Lord would put His Spirit upon them!

2. The Holy Spirit Upon The Judges of Israel:
The Book Of Judges:
        a. Othniel - 3:9-10
        b. Gideon - 6:3
        c. Jephthah - 11:29
        d. Samson - 13:24-25; 14:5-7, 19; 15:13-19

Biblical Foundation For Spiritual Growth & Maturity

2. The Holy Spirit Upon The Kings Of Israel:
   a. Saul - I Samuel 10:5-6; 9-12
   b. David - Samuel 16:13 (1-13)

4. Young Jahaziel In The Camp of Jehoshaphat
II Chronicles 20:14-20 "Then upon Jahaziel the son of Zechariah, the son of Benaiah, the son of Jeiel, the son of Mattaniah, a Levite of the sons of Asaph, came the Spirit of the LORD in the midst of the congregation. And he said: Hearken ye, all Judah, and ye inhabitants of Jerusalem, and thou king Jehoshaphat, Thus saith the LORD unto you, Be not afraid nor dismayed by reason of this great multitude; for the battle is not yours, but God's.

"Tomorrow go ye down against them: behold, they come up by the cliff of Ziz; and ye shall find them at the end of the brook before the wilderness of Jeruel. Ye shall not need to fight in this battle: set yourselves, stand ye still, and see the salvation of the LORD with you, O Judah and Jerusalem: fear not, nor be dismayed; tomorrow go out against them: for the LORD will be with you. And Jehoshaphat bowed his head with his face to the ground: and all Judah and the inhabitants of Jerusalem fell before the LORD, worshipping the LORD.

"The Levites, of the children of the Kohathites, and of the children of the Korhites, stood up to praise the LORD God of Israel with a loud voice on high.

"And they rose early in the morning and went forth into the wilderness of Tekoa: and as they went forth, Jehoshaphat stood and said: Hear me, O Judah, and ye inhabitants of Jerusalem; Believe in the LORD your God, so shall ye be established; believe his prophets, so shall ye prosper."

Old Testament Prophecy Of The Indwelling Of The Holy Spirit At Salvation

v. 25a *"Then will I sprinkle clean water upon you"* Clean water is the cleansing power of God's Word. Symbolically, water used outwardly, stands for the cleansing power of God's Word. Water used internally stands for the life-giving power of the Holy Spirit.

This context speaks of the power of God's word to deliver, heal, cleanse, and give life to the sinner from spiritual death, bondage, and enslavement. J*ohn 3:5 "Jesus answered, verily, verily I say unto thee: except a man be born of water and of the Spirit, he cannot enter into the kingdom of God. John 15:3 "Now ye are clean through the word which I have spoken unto you."*

v. 26 "A new heart also will I give you, and a new spirit will I put within you: and I will take away the stony heart out of your flesh, and I will give you an heart of flesh." – This Means "Recreation of the Human Spirit" Or To "Be Born Again" John 3:5; I Corinthians 5:17-21

v. 27a "I Will Put My Spirit Within You" – This refers to the Holy Spirit indwelling the new Christian at Salvation. The purpose of the indwelling Holy Spirit is to Revive, Give Life, Spiritual and Physical Empowerment.

v. 27b "And Cause You To Walk In My Statutes, And Ye Shall Keep My Judgments, And Do Them." This is to enable the Believer to walk in Obedience to God's Statutes, Ordinances, and Live a Transformed life
- Keep God's judgments and do them
- Abide in Christ Jesus
- Walk in obedience to God's Word and Bear Fruit

v. 28a "And ye shall dwell in the land that I gave to your fathers"- The Believer's Possession; Spiritual Inheritance and Physical Prosperity – Romans 8; Colossians 1:12-14; I Corinthians 2:1-16

v. 28b "Ye Shall Be My People, And I Will Be Your God
– Ephesians 1,2; John 1:11,12; I Corinthians 1, 2, 3, 6; Galatians; II Corinthians 5:17-21

v. 29 "I Will Also Save You From All Uncleanness: Cleansing of all sins and iniquity through the Blood of Jesus. *I John 1:8-10 "If we say that we have no sin, we deceive* ourselves, and the truth is not in us. If we confess our sins, he is faithful and just to forgive us our sins, and to cleanse us from all unrighteousness."

v. 30 The Promise Of Prosperity For The Believer: "...and I will call for the corn, and will increase it, and lay no famine upon you. And I will multiply the fruit of the tree, and the increase of the field, that ye shall receive no more reproach of famine among the heathen."

Old Testament Prophecy Of The Baptism Of The Holy Spirit (The Holy Spirit Coming UPON The Believer)

Joel 2:28-32 Amplified - *"And afterward I will pour out My Spirit upon all flesh; and your sons and your daughters shall prophesy, your old men shall dream dreams, your young men shall see visions. Even upon the menservants and upon the maidservants in those days will I pour out My Spirit. And I will show signs and wonders in the heavens, and on the earth, blood and fire and columns of smoke. The sun shall be turned to darkness and the moon to blood before the great and terrible day of the Lord comes.*

"And whoever shall call on the name of the Lord shall be delivered and saved, for in Mount Zion and in Jerusalem there shall be those who escape, as the Lord has said, and among the remnant [of survivors] shall be those whom the Lord calls."

Fulfillment Of Joel's Prophecy - Acts 2

"And when the day of Pentecost was fully come, they were all with one accord in one place. And suddenly there came a sound from heaven as of a rushing mighty wind, and it filled all the house where they were sitting. And there appeared unto them cloven tongues like as of fire, and it sat upon each of them. And they were all filled with the Holy Ghost, and began to speak with other tongues, as the Spirit gave them utterance. And there were dwelling at Jerusalem Jews, devout men, out of every nation under heaven. Now when this was noised abroad, the multitude came together and were confounded, because that every man heard them speak in his own language. And they were all amazed and marvelled, saying one to another, Behold, are not all these which speak Galilaeans?

"And how hear we every man in our own tongue, wherein we were born? Parthians, and Medes, and Elamites, and the dwellers in Mesopotamia, and in Judaea, and Cappadocia, in Pontus, and Asia, Phrygia, and Pamphylia, in Egypt, and in the parts of Libya about Cyrene, and strangers of Rome, Jews and proselytes, Cretes and Arabians, we do hear them speak in our tongues the wonderful works of God. And they were all amazed, and were in doubt, saying one to another, what meaneth this? Others mocking said, these men are full of new wine.

"But Peter, standing up with the eleven, lifted up his voice, and said unto them, Ye men of Judaea, and all ye that dwell at Jerusalem, be this known unto you, and hearken to my words: For these are not drunken, as ye suppose, seeing it is but the third hour of the day. But this is that which was spoken by the prophet Joel:

"And it shall come to pass in the last days, saith God, I will pour out of my Spirit upon all flesh: and your sons and your daughters shall prophesy, and your young men shall see visions, and your old men shall dream dreams: And on my servants and on my handmaidens, I will pour out in those days of my Spirit; and they shall prophesy: And I will shew wonders in heaven above, and signs in the earth beneath; blood, and fire, and vapor of smoke: The sun shall be turned into darkness, and the moon into blood, before the great and notable day of the Lord come: And it shall come to pass, that whosoever shall call on the name of the Lord shall be saved... Now when they heard this, they were pricked in their heart, and said unto Peter and to the rest of the apostles, Men, and brethren, what shall we do?

"Then Peter said unto them, Repent, and be baptized every one of you in the name of Jesus Christ for the remission of sins, and ye shall receive the gift of the Holy Ghost. For the promise is unto you, and to your children, and to all that are afar off, even as many as the LORD our God shall call. And with many other words did he testify and exhort, saying, save yourselves from this untoward generation. Then they that gladly received his word were baptized: and the same day there were added unto them about three thousand souls. And they continued steadfastly in the apostles' doctrine and fellowship, and in breaking of bread, and in prayers.

"And fear came upon every soul: and many wonders and signs were done by the apostles. And all that believed were together and had all things common; and sold their possessions and goods, and parted them to all men, as every man had need. And they, continuing daily with one accord in the temple, and breaking bread from house to house, did eat their meat with gladness and singleness of heart, praising God, and having favor with all the people. And the Lord added to the church daily such as should be saved."

Prophecies About The Baptism Of The Holy Spirit In The New Testament

- **Matthew 3:11-12** *"I indeed baptize you with water unto repentance: but he that cometh after me is mightier than I, whose shoes I am not worthy to bear he shall baptize you with the Holy Ghost, and with fire: Whose fan is in his hand, and he will throughly purge his floor, and gather his wheat into the garner; but he will burn up the chaff with unquenchable fire."*

- **John 7:37 -39** *"In the last day, that great day of the feast, Jesus stood and cried, saying, If any man thirst, let him come unto me, and drink. He that believeth on me, as the scripture hath said, out of his belly shall flow rivers of living water. (But this spake he of the Spirit, which they that believe on him should receive. For the Holy Ghost was not yet given; because that Jesus was not yet glorified.)"*

- **Luke 24:49** *"And behold, I send the promise of my Father upon you: but tarry ye in the city of Jerusalem, until ye be endued with power from on high."*

- ***Mark 16:15-20*** *"And these signs shall follow them that believe; In my name shall they cast out devils;* ***they shall speak with new tongues;*** *They shall take up serpents; and if they drink any deadly thing, it shall not hurt them; they shall lay hands on the sick, and they shall recover.*

- **Other References:** John 4: 7:37-39; 14:16-18,26; 15; 26; 16:7-15; 14:15-18; 26, 15:6-27; 16:5-15

The Fulfillment Of The Baptism Of The Holy Spirit In The New Testament

1. **The Early Church**
   Acts 1:4, 5, 8; 2:1-47; 4:24-37; 5:12-16

2. **Philip In Samaria** - Acts 8:4-25

3. **Cornelius And His Household** - Acts 10:1-48

4. **Believers At Ephesus** - Acts 19:1-7

The Purpose of The Holy Spirit Baptism

1. Empowers The Believer To Become An Ardent Witness of Jesus Christ - *Acts 1:8 "But ye shall receive power, after that the Holy Ghost is come upon you: and ye shall be witnesses unto me both in Jerusalem, and in all Judaea, and in Samaria, and unto the uttermost part of the earth."*

2. Communicate with the Father *I Corinthians 12:2a "For he that speaketh in an unknown tongue speaketh not unto men, but unto God"*

3. Speaks Mysteries - *I Corinthians 12:2b "For no one understands or catches his meaning, because in the Holy Spirit he utters Mysteries - secret truths and hidden things not obvious to the understanding"*

4. Edification & Release Of Spiritual Gifts *I Corinthians 12:4a "He that speaketh in an unknown tongue edifies himself"* To uplift, enlighten, motivate, build, establish, inform; improve,

5. To Know The Mind Of The Father And What He Has Freely Given To Us - *I Corinthians 2:12 "Now we have received, not the spirit of the world, but the spirit which is of God; that we might know the things that are freely given to us of God."*

6. For Spiritual Up-Building *Jude 20 Amplified "But you, beloved, building yourselves up founded on your most holy faith: [make progress, rise like an edifice higher and higher], praying in the Holy Spirit."*

7. To Help Our Infirmities (Weakness) *Romans 8:26-28 Amplified Bible "So too the Holy Spirit comes to our aid and bears us up in our weakness; for we do not know what prayer to offer nor how to offer it worthily as we ought, but the Spirit Himself goes to meet our supplication and pleads in our behalf with unspeakable yearnings and groaning too deep for utterance. And He Who searches the hearts of men knows what is in the mind of the Holy Spirit what His intent is, because the Spirit intercedes and pleads before God in behalf of the saints according to and in harmony with God's will."*

8. To Manifest The Spiritual Gifts – I Corinthians 12 & *Acts 19:5,6 "When they heard this, they were baptized in*

the name of the Lord Jesus. And when Paul had laid his hands upon them, the Holy Ghost came on them; and they spake with tongues and prophesied."

9. As A Heavenly Language For The Recreated Spirit For The Purpose Of Prayer – Romans 8:24-27; I Corinthians 2:1-16

Receive The Baptism Of The Holy Spirit

1. Accept What The Bible Teaches On The Holy Spirit And The Baptism of The Holy Spirit Without Doubt

II Timothy 3:16,17 *"All scripture is given by inspiration of God, and is profitable for doctrine, for reproof, for correction, for instruction in righteousness: That the man of God may be perfect, thoroughly furnished unto all good works.*

Mark 16:15-20 *"Go ye into all the world and preach the gospel to every creature. He that believeth and is baptized shall be saved; but he that believeth not shall be damned. And these signs shall follow them that believe; In my name shall they cast out devils; they shall speak with new tongues; They shall take up serpents; and if they drink any deadly thing, it shall not hurt them; they shall lay hands on the sick, and they shall recover."*

Acts 2:35-41 *"Now when they heard this, they were pricked in their heart, and said unto Peter and to the rest of the apostles, Men and brethren, what shall we do? Then Peter said unto them, Repent, and be baptized every one of you in the name of Jesus Christ for the remission of sins, and ye shall receive the gift of the Holy Ghost. For the promise is unto you, and to your children, and to all that* *are afar off, even as many as the Lord our God shall call. And with many other words did he testify and exhort, saying, Save yourselves from this untoward generation. Then they that gladly received his word were baptized: and the same day there were added unto them about three thousand souls."*

2. Jesus Is The Baptizer. Believe That He Will Baptize You With The Holy Spirit & Fire. It Is The Promise Of The Father

Luke 24:49 *"And behold, I send the promise of my Father upon you: but tarry ye in the city of Jerusalem, until ye be endued with power from on high.*

"Acts 1:4,5 *"And, being assembled together with them, commanded them that they should not depart from Jerusalem, but wait for the promise of the Father, which, saith he, ye have heard of me. For John truly baptized with water; but ye shall be baptized with the Holy Ghost not many days hence."*

Matthew 3:11, 12 *"I indeed baptize you with water unto repentance: but he that cometh after me is mightier than I, whose shoes I am not worthy to bear: he shall baptize you with the Holy Ghost, and with fire: Whose fan is in his hand, and he will thoroughly purge his floor, and gather his wheat into the garner; but he will burn up the chaff with unquenchable fire"*

Luke 11:9-13 *"And I say unto you, Ask, and it shall be given you; seek, and ye shall find; knock, and it shall be opened unto you. For everyone that asketh receiveth; and he that seeketh findeth; and to him that knocketh it shall be opened.*

"If a son shall ask bread of any of you that is a father, will he give him a stone? or if he ask a fish, will he for a fish give him a serpent? Or if he shall ask an egg, will he offer him a scorpion? If ye then, being evil, know how to give good gifts unto your children: how much more shall your heavenly Father give the Holy Spirit to them that ask him?

3. Ask God To Forgive You Of Your Known Sins And Believe You Are Forgiven 1 John 1:8-10

4. Renounce Every Involvement In Any Form Of Satanism - Cult, Occult, Witchcraft, And Any Lifestyle, Which Contradicts The Word Of God. - Acts 8:1-17

5. Ask For The Baptism Of The Holy Spirit In Faith. Do Not Limit Yourself Or God With Any Your Mental Reasoning Or Unbelief. Simply Believe And Follow The Leadership Of The Holy Spirit - *Luke 11:13 "If you then, who are evil, know how to give good gifts to your children, how much more will the heavenly Father give the Holy Spirit to those who ask him!"*

6. Open Your Heart. Eagerly Pursue, Seek, Receive The Baptism Of The Holy Spirit. *I Cor. 12:31 The Amplified Bible "Make it your aim, your greatest desire receive spiritual endowments - But earnestly desire and strive for the greater gifts [if acquiring them is going to be your goal]. And yet I will show you a still more excellent way [one of the choicest graces and the highest of them all: unselfish love]."*

7. Make Time For Prayer. Wait On The Lord. "Tarry Ye Until" - Luke 24:49; Acts 2; Acts 4:24: Psalm 27

This Statement Is Profound: It is Loaded. Whereas I do not want to sound like I am propounding a dogmatic theory, I would like to emphasize that the phrase "Tarry Until" brings into the equation a sense of focus, urgency, dedication, commitment, and the decision to wait or patiently endure till you receive what you are looking for. Quitting before the manifestation is not an option.

THE WORD "TARRY" MEANS:
- To delay or linger in expectation of…
- To abide or stay in or at a place until your expectation is granted (fulfilled). It carries with it the idea of serious and conscious consideration. An Expectation without doubting; or achieving an aim in patience and persistence.

Luke 24:49 "And behold, I send the promise of my Father upon you: but tarry ye in the city of Jerusalem, until ye be endued with power from on high."

Acts 1:4, 5 "And, being assembled together with them, commanded them that they should not depart from Jerusalem, but wait for the promise of the Father which, saith he, ye have heard of me. For John truly baptized with water; but ye shall be baptized with the Holy Ghost not many days hence."

8. **Fast If Necessary - Fasting Will Help Prepare Your Spirit, Souls, And Body To Be More Receptive To The Infilling Or Baptism Of The Holy Spirit.**

Joel 2:10-17; 28,29 *"Therefore also now, saith the LORD, turn ye even to me with all your heart, and with fasting, and with weeping, and with mourning: And rend your heart, and not your garments, and turn unto the LORD your God:*

"For he is gracious and merciful, slow to anger, and of great kindness, and repenteth him of the evil...

"Blow the trumpet in Zion, sanctify a fast, call a solemn assembly: Gather the people, sanctify the congregation, assemble the elders, gather the children, and those that suck the breasts: Let the bridegroom go forth of his chamber, and the bride out of her closet. Let the priests, the ministers of the LORD, weep between the porch and the altar, and let them say: Spare thy people, O LORD, and give not thine heritage to reproach, that the heathen should rule over them: wherefore should they say among the people: Where is their God?"

Isaiah 58:6-14 *"Is not this the fast that I have chosen? To lose the bands of wickedness, to undo the heavy burdens, and to let the oppressed go free, and that ye break every yoke? Is it not to deal thy bread to the hungry, and that thou bring the poor that are cast out to thy house? when thou seest the naked, that thou cover him; and that thou hide not thyself from thine own flesh? Then shall thy light break forth as the morning, and thine health shall spring forth speedily: and thy righteousness shall go before thee; the glory of the LORD shall be thy rereward.*

"Then shalt thou call, and the LORD shall answer; thou shalt cry, and he shall say, here I am. If thou take away from the midst of thee the yoke, the putting forth of the finger, and speaking vanity. And if thou draw out thy soul to the hungry and satisfy the afflicted soul; then shall thy light rise in obscurity, and thy darkness be as the noon day: And the LORD shall guide thee continually, and satisfy thy soul in drought, and make fat thy bones: and thou shalt be like a watered garden, and like a spring of water, whose waters fail not.

"And they that shall be of thee shall build the old waste places: thou shalt raise up the foundations of many generations; and thou shalt be called, The repairer of the breach, The restorer of paths to dwell in. If thou turn away thy foot from the sabbath, from doing thy pleasure on my holy day; and call the sabbath a delight, the holy of the LORD, honorable; and shalt honour him, not doing thine own ways, nor finding thine own pleasure, nor speaking thine own words: Then shalt thou delight thyself in the LORD; and I will cause thee to ride upon the high places of the earth and feed thee."

SPECIAL NOTE! - Jesus Christ is the sole Baptizer of the Holy Spirit (Ghost) and fire. Pastors, Church leaders, and any other person who offers to help are only channels for God. This means if there is no one available to assist you, you can pray for yourself. Do not try to copy the tongues (it is not a good practice to literally imitate or teach someone how to speak in tongues).

STUDY LESSON IIII
THE BAPTISM OF THE HOLY SPIRIT

Define The Following

1. Tarry _____

_____

2. Endued With Power _____

_____

3. Witnesses _____

_____

4. In Your Own Words, What Does The Following Scripture References Mean? (Joel 2:28,29 and Acts 2:1-4)

_____

_____

_____

_____

_____

_____

_____

_____

The Christian Foundation

Mark 16:15-20 (Review from Lesson III)

1. To Whom Did Jesus Commission His Disciples To Preach? _____

2. These Signs Shall Follow Believers:
   a) _____

   b) _____

   c) _____

   d) _____

The Holy Spirit

1. Define Holy Spirit Baptism. _____

_____

_____

_____

2. What Is The Initial Evidence Of Holy Spirit Baptism? _

_____

3. Describe The Following Symbols Of The Holy Spirit.

Dove _____

Eagle _____

Biblical Foundation For Spiritual Growth & Maturity

Fire _____

Cloud, water, river _____

Oil, butter, light _____

The Holy Spirit In The Old Testament

For What Purpose Did The Holy Spirit Come Upon The Following In The Old Testament?

a. Moses And The Seventy Elders _____

_____

_____

b. The judges of Israel:

Othniel _____

Gideon _____

Jephthah _____

Samson _____

Saul _____

David _____

2. Explain The Old Testament Prophecy Of The Indwelling Of The Holy Spirit _____

3. Explain the Old Testament Prophecy of the baptism of the Holy Spirit. _____

_____

The Holy Spirit In The New Testament

1. Comment Briefly On What Each Of The Following Said About The Holy Spirit:

John the Baptist _____

Mark _____

Apostle John _____

Saint Luke _____
Saint Luke on the fulfillment of the Baptism of the Holy Spirit in the book of Luke and Acts of the Apostles: List at least five purposes served by the Holy Spirit Baptism. Give specific scriptures to support each purpose.

a) _____

    Scripture _____

b) _____

    Scripture _____

c) _____

    Scripture _____

Biblical Foundation For Spiritual Growth & Maturity

d) _____

   Scripture _____

e) _____

   Scripture _____

3. Briefly Comment On The Seven Steps To Receiving The Baptism Of The Holy Spirit.

a) _____

b) _____

c) _____

d) _____

e) _____

f) _____

g) _____

h) _____

_____

_____

_____

Review Questions

1. What is Holy Spirit Baptism? _____

_____

_____

2. What is the initial evidence of the Holy Spirit Baptism?

_____

3. What purposes does the Holy Spirit serve? _____

_____

_____

_____

_____

4. **Matthew 3:11** Speaks of baptism in water and in the Holy Ghost. Acts 2:38: "Then Peter said unto them, Repent, and be baptized every one of you in the name of Jesus Christ for the remission of sins, and ye shall receive the gift of the Holy Ghost." Develop a detailed statement bringing all of these scriptures together. Use a separate sheet if needed

_____

_____

Biblical Foundation For Spiritual Growth & Maturity

5. What impact does this chapter have on the ministry for which God has called us today?

Challenge Questions

Why did the Holy Spirit, only empowered a few for a specific purpose in the Old Testament? Write a prescription for receiving the baptism of the Holy Spirit. What is the difference between the anointing of the Holy Spirit and the Baptism of the Holy Spirit? Use separate sheet.

The Gifts Of The Holy Spirit

Hebrews 2:1-4 "Therefore we ought to give the more earnest heed to the things which we have heard, lest at any time we should let them slip. For if the word spoken by angels was stedfast, and every transgression and disobedience received a just recompence of reward; How shall we escape, if we neglect so great salvation; which at the first began to be spoken by the Lord, and was confirmed unto us by them that heard him; God also bearing them witness, both with signs and wonders, and with divers miracles, and gifts of the Holy Ghost, according to his own will?"

Chapter 4
The Gifts Of The Holy Spirit

The gifts of the Holy Spirit are a set of attributes or manifestations of the Holy Spirit's power and authority in the lives of believers

Key Scriptures for The Gifts Of The Holy Spirit

I Corinthians 12:4-7 *"Now there are [distinctive] varieties of spiritual gifts [special abilities given by the grace and extraordinary power of the Holy Spirit operating in believers], but it is the same Spirit [who grants them and empowers believers].*

"And there are [distinctive] varieties of ministries and service, but it is the same Lord [who is served]. And there are [distinctive] ways of working [to accomplish things], but it is the same God who produces all things in all believers [inspiring, energizing, and empowering them].

"But to each one is given the manifestation of the Spirit [the spiritual illumination and the enabling of the Holy Spirit] for the common good" The Amplified Bible

Acts 1:8 *"But ye shall receive power, after that the Holy Ghost is come upon you: and ye shall be witnesses unto me both in Jerusalem, and in all Judaea, and in Samaria, and unto the uttermost part of the earth."*

Mark 16:15-20 *"And he said unto them, Go ye into all the world, and preach the gospel to every creature He that believeth and is baptized shall be saved; but he that believeth not shall be damned.*

"And these signs shall follow them that believe; In my name shall they cast out devils; they shall speak with new tongues.

"They shall take up serpents; and if they drink any deadly thing, it shall not hurt them; they shall lay hands on the sick, and they shall recover.

"So then after the Lord had spoken unto them, he was received up into heaven, and sat on the right hand of God. And they went forth, and preached everywhere, the Lord working with them, and confirming the word with signs following. Amen.

Strategic Divisions Of The Gifts of The Holy Spioriot

1. There Are **Diversities of Gifts** but the same Spirit
2. **Differences of Administrations** but the same Lord
3. **Diversities of Operations** but it is the same God who works in all. The Manifestation of the Spirit is given to every Man to profit withal.

The Nine Gifts Of The Holy Spirit
1 Corinthians 12:1-9

1. The Gift Of Word Of Wisdom
2. The Gifts Of Word Of Knowledge
3. The Gift Of Faith
4. The Gifts of Healings
5. The Working of Miracles
6. Prophecy
7. Discerning of Spirits
8. Divers kinds of tongues
9. The interpretation of Tongues

Three Divisions Of The Manifestations Of The Holy Spirit - (Corinthians 12:4)

1. Gifts (Divine Endowment Or Faculty) - God has given to the Church (this dispensation of Grace) a threefold manifestation of the Prophetic Gifts:
    a) Prophecy - Inspired utterance
    b) Diverse kinds of Tongues
    c) Interpretation of Tongues

2. Administration (1 Corinthians 12:5) - The Act Of Managing Duties, Responsibilities, Rules: Administering
    a) Word of Knowledge.
    b) Word of Wisdom.
    c) Discerning of Spirit

3. Operations (1 Corinthians 12:6)
    a) Faith
    b) The Workings Of Miracles
    c) Gifts of Healing

Ten Ministries Of The Holy Spirit

1. Glorifies Jesus - 1 Corinthians 1:3; John 16:13-14
2. Inspires Manifestations - 1 Corinthians 12:7, 11
3. Forms the Body of Christ - 1 Corinthians 12: 13
4. Energizes The Believer - 1 Corinthians 13 v.13
5. Imparts love - 1 Corinthians 13:1-13; Romans 5:5
6. Reveals Mysteries to the recreated spirit - 1 Corinthians 12:10; 14:2, 13-19, 21-23, 26-28
7. Interprets mysteries of tongues - 1 Cor.12:10; 14:5
8. Edifies by Prophecy - 1 Cor. 14:3-31
9. Edifies Believers in tongues - 1 Cor. 4:4
10. Gives Gifts to Believers - 1 Cor. 12:8-10; Rom. 12:6

Defining The Gifts Of The Holy Spirit

I Corinthians 12:8-11
- *To one is given through the [Holy] Spirit [the power to speak] the **message of wisdom***
- *To another [the power to express] the **word of knowledge and understanding** according to the same Spirit*
- *To another [wonder-working] **Faith** [is given] by the same [Holy] Spirit,*
- *To another the [extraordinary] **Gifts of Healings** by the one Spirit.*
- *To another the working of **Miracles**,*
- *To another **Prophecy** [foretelling the future, speaking a new message from God to the people],*
- *To another **Discernment Of Spirits** [the ability to distinguish sound, godly doctrine from the deceptive doctrine of man-made religions and cults],*
- *To another **Various Kinds Of [Unknown] Tongues**,*
- *To another **Interpretation Of Tongues.** All these things [the gifts, the achievements, the abilities, the empowering] are brought about by one and the same [Holy] Spirit, distributing to each one individually just as He chooses."*

I - Gifts of Revelation

- **The Word of Wisdom** - This is supernatural revelation, or insight into God's divine Will, Counsel, and Purpose, showing how to solve any problem that may arise - 1 Kings 3:16-28; Matt. 2:20; Luke 22:10-12; John 2:22-24; 4:16-19; Acts 26:16; 27:21-25; 1 Corinthians 5

- **The Word of Knowledge** - This is supernatural revelation of divine knowledge, or insight into God's Wisdom, Counsel, Mind as pertaining to His. Will, Purpose, and Plan; also, that of man that could not be known by physical means - Gen. 1:1-2:25; 1 Sam. 3:7-15; 2 Kings 6:8-12; Acts 9:11-12; Matt. 16:16; Acts 5:3-4; 21;11; Ephesus 3

- **Discerning of Spirits** - This is supernatural revelation or insight into the realm of the spirits to expose their plans, schemes, strategy, purpose, etc.

  This gift does not only discern the world of Satan but also the realm and activity of angels of light as well as the Holy Spirit. Matt. 9:4; Luke 13:16; John 2:25; Acts 13:9-10; 16:16; 1 Timothy 4:1-4; 1 John 4:1-6

II - Gifts of Inspiration

- **Prophecy** – A Supernatural, inspired utterance for edification, exhortation, comfort. Inspired declaration of divine of God's purpose. Prediction of something to come. Acts 3:21; 21:11; 2 Pt. 1:21; 1 Cor. 14:3, 23-32

- **Diverse Kinds Of Tongues** - This is a supernatural utterance in a known language, which is not known to the speaker. Isaiah 28:11; Mk 16:17; Acts 2; 1 Cor. 12

- **The Interpretation Of Tongues** - This is a supernatural ability to interpret in the native tongue what is uttered in the spirit. 1 Corinthians 12

III - Gifts Of Power (Working Gifts)

- **Faith** - This is a supernatural ability to believe God without human doubt, unbelief, and reasoning. Rom. 4; James 1; Matt 8; Matt. 17:20; 21:22; Mark 9:23; 11:22-24; Heb. 11:2,6; 12:1-3

- **The Gifts Of Healings** - This is a supernatural power to heal all manner of sickness, disease, afflictions, etc. without human, medical / scientific or native help. Mk 16:15-20; John 14:12; 1 Cor. 12

- **The Working Of Miracles** - The supernatural ability/power to intervene in the ordinary course of nature and to counteract natural laws if necessary. Examples: The man with a withered hand; The woman with an issue of blood; Jarius daughter raised from the dead; Blind Bartimeaus; The crippled man at the beautiful gate.

FACTS ON MANIFESTING THE GIFTS
- Every Christian has the Holy Spirit dwelling him
- The Baptism of the Holy Spirit empowers the believer for worship and service
- Personal Devotion - consistent prayer, study of God's word, fasting, consecration, love and compassion, intercessory prayer and life of faith prepares and establishes the believer for the manifestation of spiritual gifts.

STUDY LESSON: IV
THE GIFTS OF THE HOLY SPIRIT

Memory Reference

In Your Own Words, Explain Gifts of the Spirit And Fruit Of The Spirit

_____

_____

_____

_____

_____

_____

The Holy Spirit

The Holy Spirit within is _____

The Holy Spirit upon is _____

List And Explain, Using The Scriptural References, The Ten Ministries Of The Holy Spirit. Use Separate Sheet If Necessary.

_____

_____

_____

_____

_____

The Christian Foundation

Faith is listed as a fruit of the Holy Spirit and a gift of the Holy Spirit. Explain the difference. Use Separate sheet

_____

_____

_____

Below is a list of the Gifts of the Spirit. Beside each gift, list the Divisions of the Manifestations and type of gifts.

Divisions of the Manifestations   **Type of Gifts**

a) Divine endowment or faculty   d) Revelation
b) Administration   e) Inspiration
c) Operations   f) Working Gifts

                                                Divisions   Type of
Gift

1) The Gift Of Word Of Wisdom   _____ _____

2) The Gifts Of Word Of Knowledge _____ _____

3) Faith   _____ _____

4) The Gifts of Healings   _____ _____

5) The Working of Miracle   _____ _____

Biblical Foundation For Spiritual Growth & Maturity

Gift

6) Prophecy _____ _____

7) Discerning of Spirits _____ _____

8) Divers Kinds of Tongues _____ _____

9) The Interpretation of Tongues _____ _____

Challenge Questions

1. Choose five gifts of the Holy Spirit and sight specific Biblical examples of each: Use Separate Sheet If Necessary.

a) _____

_____

_____

_____

b) _____

_____

_____

c) _____

_____

d) _____

e) _____

Expound on the necessity of the gifts of the Holy Spirit in the life of the twenty-first century Believer. Also Briefly Define the difference between the Five-fold Office of the Holy Spirit and the Gifts of the Holy Spirit. Use Separate Sheet If Necessary.

Biblical Foundation For Spiritual Growth & Maturity

Fruit Of The Recreated Spirit

Galatians 5:16 -26 "This I say then: Walk in the Spirit, and ye shall not fulfill the lust of the flesh. For the flesh lusteth against the Spirit, and the Spirit against the flesh: and these are contrary the one to the other: so that ye cannot do the things that ye would. But if ye be led of the Spirit, ye are not under the law."

Chapter 5
Fruit Of The Recreated Spirit

Fruit bearing identifies the Christian with the Savior. It is the very nature and character of God the world is looking for."

Key Scriptures On The Christian & Fruit Bearing

John 15:1-5 *"I am the true vine, and my Father is the husbandman. Every branch in me that beareth not fruit he taketh away: and every branch that beareth fruit, he purgeth it, that it may bring forth more fruit. Now ye are clean through the word which I have spoken unto you. Abide in me, and I in you. As the branch cannot bear fruit of itself, except it abide in the vine; no more can ye, except ye abide in me. I am the vine, ye are the branches: He that abideth in me, and I in him, the same bringeth forth much fruit: for without me ye can do nothing."*

Matthew 3:8 *"Bring forth therefore fruits meet for repentance"*

Matthew 7:16 - 20 *"Ye shall know them by their fruits. Do men gather grapes of thorns, or figs of thistles? Even so every good tree bringeth forth good fruit; but a corrupt tree bringeth forth, evil fruit. good tree cannot bring forth, evil fruit; neither can a corrupt tree bring forth good fruit. Every tree that bringeth not forth good fruit is hewn down and cast into the fire. Wherefore by their fruits ye shall know them."*

Galatians 5:1,16-18 *"Stand fast therefore in the liberty wherewith Christ hath made us free and be not entangled again with the yoke of bondage...*

"This I say then: Walk in the Spirit, and ye shall not fulfill the lust of the flesh. For the flesh lusteth against the Spirit, and the Spirit against the flesh: and these are contrary the one to the other: so that ye cannot do the things that ye would. But if ye be led of the Spirit, ye are not under the law" **John 15:16** *"Ye have not chosen me, but I have chosen you, and ordained you, that ye should go and bring forth fruit, and that your fruit should remain, that whatsoever ye shall ask of the Father in my name, he may give it you."* **Matthew 12:33** *"Either make the tree good, and his fruit good; or else make the tree corrupt, and his fruit corrupt: for the tree is known by his fruit."*

The Works (Fruit) Of The Flesh - *Galatians 5:19-21*
"Now the works of the flesh are manifest, which are these; Adultery, fornication, uncleanness, lasciviousness, Idolatry, witchcraft, hatred, variance, emulations, wrath, strife, seditions, heresies, Envyings, murders, drunkenness, revellings, and such like: Of the which I tell you before, as I have also told you in time past, that they which do such things shall not inherit the kingdom of God.

The Works Of The Flesh:
1. Adultery & Fornication
2. Uncleanness,
3. Lasciviousness
4. Idolatry & Witchcraft
5. Hatred & Variance
6. Emulations
7. Wrath, Strife & Seditions
8. Heresies & Envying
9. Murders
10. Drunkenness & reveling

The Fruit Of The Recreated Spirit - *"But the fruit of the Spirit is love, joy, peace, longsuffering, gentleness, goodness, faith, Meekness, temperance: against such there is no law.*

"And they that are Christ's have crucified the flesh with the affections and lusts. If we live in the Spirit, let us also walk in the Spirit. Let us not be desirous of vain glory, provoking one another, envying one another."

The Fruit Of The Recreated Spirit:
1. Love
2. Joy
3. Peace
4. Long-suffering
5. Gentleness
6. Goodness
7. Faith
8. Meekness
9. Temperance

1. Love (Greek Agapao or Agape - Noun) - God's Love

Biblical Definitions (Greek & Hebrew)
a. **Agape (Greek):** Unconditional, selfless love, often associated with God's love for humanity - John 3:16; 1 Corinthians 13:1-3
b. **Phileo (Greek):** Brotherly love, affection, or friendship, often used to describe human relationships (John 21:15-17; Romans 12:10
c. **Chesed (Hebrew):** Loving-kindness, mercy, or compassion, often used to describe God's love and faithfulness - Psalm 136:1-3; Isaiah 54:10

The Characteristics of Love
a. **True Love is Selflessness:** Love is characterized by selflessness, putting the needs and interests of others before one's own - 1 Corinthians 13:5
b. **True Love is Unconditional**: God's Love (Agape), is unconditional, accepting and loving others without discrimination, expectation of reward or reciprocation Matthew 5:44-45
c. **True Love is Sacrificial:** Willing to make sacrifices for the benefit of others, demonstrating its depth and commitment - John 15:13
d. **True Love** Forgiving: Love is forgiving, letting go of grudges and resentments, and seeking reconciliation and healing - Matthew 6:14-15

Cultivating Love
a. **Prayer: According to** *Romans 5:5b: "God's love has been poured into our hearts through the Holy Spirit which has been given to us."* - Ask the Holy Spirit to manifest this Love through Prayer. Ask God to fill you with His Love and Compassion - 1 Corinthians 13:1-3
b. **By Personal Evaluation:** Self-Reflection: Engage in self-reflection, recognizing areas where you can grow in love and demonstrate it to others - 1 Cor. 13:4-7
c. **By Selflessly** Serving and being Kind to others, especially those in need. Show love through service. Put the needs of others before your own; demonstrate Kindness and Compassion - Galatians 5:13-14
d. **By Fellowship** – Do not forget the Assembling of the Brethren (Believers). Surround yourself with a supportive community, sharing Love, Compassion, and encouraging one another - Hebrews 10:24-25

1. Joy

Joy Is A Profound, Multifaceted Emotion That Encompasses Happiness, Delight, Contentment. From a Biblical perspective, joy is a fruit of the recreated Spirit of Man, - Galatians 5:22, and a fundamental aspect of the Christian life.

The Greek Word for Joy is Chara. It implies Joy, Gladness, or Delight, often associated with God's presence and blessings - Psalm 16:11; Luke 1:47.

The Hebrew "Simchah" Is Also: Joy, Gladness, Or Rejoicing, often linked to celebrations, worship, and God's goodness Psalm 100:1-5; Isaiah 61:10.

The Biblical Characteristics of Joy

a. **Inner Peace:** Joy is rooted in inner peace, which comes from trusting in God's Sovereignty and Goodness - Philippians 4:7

b. **Gratitude:** Joy is often accompanied by gratitude, recognizing and appreciating God's blessings and provisions (1 Thessalonians 5:18).

c. **Hope:** Joy is fueled by hope, trusting in God's promises and looking forward to His future plans. - Rom. 5:2-5

d. **Worship:** Joy is expressed through worship, acknowledging and celebrating God's greatness and majesty - Psalm 100:1-5.

Cultivating Joy:

As a Believer, you can cultivate God's Joy in your life. The following are ways to activating and releasing Joy within us:

a. **By Prayer**: Pray, asking God to manifest His Presence and Joy in you. - John 16:24

b. **By Gratefulness and Gratitude**: Be Grateful, Practice Gratitude, regularly reflecting on God's blessings and provisions - 1 Thessalonians 5:18

c. **By Worship and Praise**: Engage God in in Worship and Praise, celebrating God's Goodness and Greatness - Psalm 100:1-5.

d. **By Fellowship** – Do not forget the Assembling of the Brethren (Believers). Surround yourself with a supportive community, sharing joy and encouraging one another. - Hebrews 10:24-25

2. Peace

Peace: God is Peace. This is not the Peace of the World. It's a Divine Gift and a Human Pursuit. From a Biblical perspective, peace is considered a divine gift and a fundamental aspect of human flourishing.

Biblical Definition

a. **Shalom (Hebrew):** Wholeness, completeness, or peace, often used to describe a state of well-being, harmony, and prosperity - Psalm 29:11; Jeremiah 29:11

b. **Eirene (Greek):** Peace, tranquility, or harmony, often used to describe a state of inner calm and outer stability John 14:27; Romans 5:1

The Characteristics of Peace
a. **Inner Calm:** Peace is characterized by inner calm, serenity, and tranquility, even in the midst of chaos or uncertainty (Philippians 4:7).

b. **Harmony:** Peace involves harmony and balance in relationships, whether personal, social, or spiritual (Matthew 5:23-24).

c. **Wholeness:** Peace encompasses a sense of wholeness and completeness, where all aspects of life are integrated and aligned (Psalm 138:8).

d. **Forgiveness:** Peace is often linked to forgiveness, letting go of grudges and resentments, and seeking reconciliation and healing (Matthew 6:14-15).

How To Cultivate & Manifest God's Peace
a. **By Prayer:** Seek peace through prayer, asking God to manifest through you His Peace and Presence Philippians 4:6-7

b. **By Mindfulness:** Live with the Consciousness and Practice of God's Peace in You. Always focus on God's Presence in You, that you received at Salvation. Do not allow the present moment to depress you. Endeavor to let go of worries about the past or future Matthew 6:34

c. **By Forgiveness:** Embrace God's forgiveness. Cultivate and always practice forgiveness, recognizing that holding onto grudges and resentments can disrupt peace and harmony- Matthew 6:14-15

d. **By Fellowship**: Jesus Prayed that: "All Will Be One". Surround yourself with a supportive people, sharing peace and encouragement with others – Hebrews 10:24-25

3. **Long-Suffering** - Consistent, Quite and Aggressive, Long and Patient Endurance, irrespective of any prevailing circumstance or offense.

4. **Gentleness - Humbleness, Humility** - The quality or state of being gentle; mildness of manners or disposition. Philippians 2:15-13 - The Mind of Humility, Servanthood, and Obedience.

5. **Goodness** - The quality or state of being and doing what is right

6. **Faith** in Biblical context is the firm, uncompromising trust, belief, hope that looks forward to achieving positive result or outcome even when there is no tangible, physical proof. It is the ability to completely rely on God's Word. It is also believing that whatever He (God) has promised, He is able also to Perform. It is the Title Deed; the Substance of things hoped for and thew evidence of things not seen - Hebrews 11.

7. **Meekness** - The grace, strength, and ability to endure any form of rejection, abuse, demands, character assassination, ridicule, life challenges etc. with patience without *resentment*.

8. **Temperance** - Moderation in action, thought, or feeling: (Restraint). Habitual moderation in the indulgence of the appetites or passions

Please Meditate On the Following Scriptures
The Righteous Live & Walks By Faith

Galatians 3:1-9 *"O foolish Galatians, who hath bewitched you, that ye should not obey the truth, before whose eyes Jesus Christ hath been evidently set forth, crucified among you?*

"This only would I learn of you, Received ye the Spirit by the works of the law, or by the hearing of faith? Are ye so foolish? having begun in the Spirit, are ye now made perfect by the flesh? Have ye suffered so many things in vain? if it be yet in vain. He therefore that ministereth to you the Spirit, and worketh miracles among you, doeth he it by the works of the law, or by the hearing of faith?

"Even as Abraham believed God, and it was accounted to him for righteousness. Know ye therefore that they which are of faith, the same are the children of Abraham. And the scripture, foreseeing that God would justify the heathen through faith, preached before the gospel unto Abraham, saying, In thee shall all nations be blessed. So then they which be of faith are blessed with faithful Abraham"

John 15:1-14 *"I am the true vine, and my Father is the husbandman. Every branch in me that beareth not fruit he taketh away: and every branch that beareth fruit, he purgeth it, that it may bring forth more fruit. Now ye are clean through the word which I have spoken unto you.*

"Abide in me, and I in you. As the branch cannot bear fruit of itself, except it abide in the vine; no more can ye, except ye abide in me.

"I am the vine, ye are the branches: He that abideth in me, and I in him, the same bringeth forth much fruit: for without me ye can do nothing.

"If a man abide not in me, he is cast forth as a branch, and is withered; and men gather them, and cast them into the fire, and they are burned.

"If ye abide in me, and my words abide in you, ye shall ask what ye will, and it shall be done unto you.
Joh 15:8 *Herein is my Father glorified, that ye bear much fruit; so shall ye be my disciples.*

"As the Father hath loved me, so have I loved you: continue ye in my love. If ye keep my commandments, ye shall abide in my love; even as I have kept my Father's commandments, and abide in his love.

"These things have I spoken unto you, that my joy might remain in you, and that your joy might be full. This is my commandment, That ye love one another, as I have loved you.

"Greater love hath no man than this, that a man lay down his life for his friends. Ye are my friends, if ye do whatsoever I command you."

STUDY LESSON: V
THE FRUIT OF THE RECREATED SPIRIT

1. Define and expound on the differences between the Fruit Of The Recreated Spirit and the Fruit or Works of the Flesh as found in Galatians 5 (Use separate sheet if necessary).

2. Expound On The Following Scripture: Galatians 3:1-5

3. What Is The Importance Of Bearing Fruit? How Can Fruit Bearing Reveal The Christ In You, Impact And Transform Your Community And Beyond?

4. Briefly Expound On The Following Scripture:
John 15:1-17

5. Briefly Expound on The Following Scriptures:
John 14:1-14; John 16:1-33

Deliverance & Healing

Isaiah 49:24, 25 "Shall the prey be taken from the mighty: Or the lawful captive delivered? But thus, saith the LORD: Even the captives of the mighty Shall be taken away. And the prey of the terrible shall be delivered. For I will contend with him that contendeth with thee, And I will save thy children."

Isaiah 53:2-5 "He is despised and rejected of men; a man of sorrows and acquainted with grief: and we hid as it were our faces from him; he was despised, and we esteemed him not. Surely, he hath borne our griefs, and carried our sorrows: yet we did esteem him stricken, smitten of God, and afflicted. But he was wounded for our transgressions, he was bruised for our iniquities: the chastisement of our peace was upon him; and with his stripes we are healed."

Chapter 6
Redemption, Deliverance, Healing & Restoration

Deliverance is the act of being freed from evil spirits and dark forces. It can also mean stopping sin, being freed from dark hands, and stopping Satan and demons. Some types of deliverance include repenting of sins, renouncing lawlessness, and being saved in Jesus' name.

Healing - The act of restoring, transforming, sustaining, and nurturing the whole person, including the body, mind, and spirit. It can also mean healing wounded emotions, which is called inner healing.

Restoration - The act of returning something to its former condition or making something new again. It can also mean getting back original blessings, receiving a new gift, or being promoted. "Restoration" is often used in the Bible to refer to tangible getting back life, property, health etc.

Understanding Redemption

Christ Delt With All Curses On The Cross The Believer (The Christian) Is Free From All Curses

"Christ hath redeemed us from the curse of the law, being made a curse for us: For it is written, cursed is everyone that hangeth on a tree: that the blessing of Abraham might come on the Gentiles through Jesus Christ; that we might receive the promise of the Spirit through faith." Galatians 3:13, 14 KJV

Four Greek Words Defining Redemption

1. **Agorazo (Greek) - "To Buy Out"** - It is used metaphorically in Galatians 3:13 and Galatians chapters 4 and 5 of the deliverance and healing of the bound, oppressed, diseased etc. by Christ Jesus from the Law of sin and death, iniquity, curse and whatever enslaves.

2. **Exagorazo (Greek) - "To Buy Back"** – Specifically, purchasing a slave with the intention or view of his total freedom – unshackle the shackled from all his spiritual and physical bondages, burdens, yokes, curses, attitudes, etc. Redeemed (Purchased) with the intention of total freedom.

    Colossians 1:12-14 - *"Giving thanks unto the Father, which hath "MADE US" (ENABLED US): made us meet to be partakers of the inheritance of the saints in light: Who hath delivered us from the power of darkness, and hath translated us into the Kingdom of His Dear Son. In whom we have Redemption through his blood, even the forgiveness of sins."*

3. **Lutroo (Gk) - To Release on Receipt of Ransom.** This is used in the middle voice to signify release by paying a ransom – PRICE. In this case the price is the Blood of Jesus.

    Redemption speaks of the work of Christ in buying back man from all his iniquity, lawlessness (the bondage of self-will, which rejects God's will. How did he do it?

Isaiah's Prophecy: *Isaiah 53:1-5* *"Who hath believed our report? and to whom is the arm of the LORD revealed? For he shall grow up before him as a tender plant, and as a root out of a dry ground: he hath neither form nor comeliness; and when we shall see him, there is no beauty that we should desire him.*

"He is despised and rejected of men; a man of sorrows and acquainted with grief: and we hid as it were our faces from him; he was despised, and we esteemed him not.

"Surely, he hath borne our griefs, and carried our sorrows: yet we did esteem him stricken, smitten of God, and afflicted. But he was wounded for our transgressions; he was bruised for our iniquities: the chastisement of our peace was upon him; and with his stripes we are healed." Other References: Isaiah 53:1-5; Titus 2:14; Hebrews 9:11-17

4. **Apolutrosis (Gk)** – This Word Is Used To Describe The End Result Of The Entire Transaction. This is the absolute, total emancipation: After the price is paid, the slave is no longer a slave or belongs to the former slave master, he is restored to the rightful owner (in this case, his creator, Christ Jesus).

   The former slave (Former Fallen Man) is restored to his original position of sonship, fellowship, authority, power, dominion, obedience, prosperity, and responsibility.

   References: Ephesians 2:1-10; II Corinthian 5:17-21; Ephesians 2:13-22

The Christian Foundation

Other Scriptures On The Price Christ Paid:

Christ Jesus was able, in His Humanity to go through the torture and scourging from the moment of His arrest to dying on the cross because he overcame the spiritual battle on His knees in the Garden of Gethsemane. Christ in His humanity battled every opposition and won.

1. **The Gethsemane Experience & From Gethsemane To The Crucifixion**
   Matthew 26:39-46; Matthew 26:47-75

2. **The Resurrection Experience**
   Matthew 28:1-10; Philippians 2:5-11; Ephesians 1:19-23; Revelation 1:17 -18; Romans 8:8-11

3. **Jesus Is Our Chief Advocate** - The Ascension of Jesus and His present ministry at the right hand of the Father. *- I John 2:1-3*

Key Scriptures For Deliverance, Healing & Restoration

Isaiah 49:24,25 *"Shall the prey be taken from the mighty, or the lawful captive delivered? But thus saith the LORD, Even the captives of the mighty shall be taken away, and the prey of the terrible shall be delivered: for I will contend with him that contendeth with thee, and I will save thy children.*

Isaiah 53:3-5 *"He is despised and rejected of men; a man of sorrows and acquainted with grief: and we hid as it were our faces from him; he was despised, and we esteemed him not.*

"Surely, he hath borne our griefs, and carried our sorrows: yet we did esteem him stricken, smitten of God, and afflicted. But he was wounded for our transgressions, he was bruised for our iniquities: the chastisement of our peace was upon him; and with his stripes we are healed."

II Chronicles 7:12-16 "...If my people, which are called by my name, shall humble themselves, and pray, and seek my face, and turn from their wicked ways; then will I hear from heaven, and will forgive their sin, and will heal their land. Now mine eyes shall be open, and mine ears attent unto the prayer that is made in this place. For now have I chosen and sanctified this house, that my name may be there forever: and mine eyes and mine heart shall be there perpetually."

III John 2 "Beloved, I wish above all things that thou mayest prosper and be in health even as thy soul prosper."

John 10:10,11 "The thief cometh not, but for to steal, and to kill, and to destroy. I am come that they might have life, and that they might have it more abundantly. I am the good shepherd: the good shepherd giveth his life for the sheep."

Ephesians 6:10-13 "Finally, my brethren, be strong in the Lord, and in the power of his might. Put on the whole armor of God, that ye may be able to stand against the wiles of the devil. For we wrestle not against flesh and blood, but against principalities, against powers, against the rulers of the darkness of this world, against spiritual wickedness in high places. Wherefore take unto you the whole armor of God, that ye may be able to withstand in the evil day, and having done all, to stand."

Key Tools Satan Uses To Encroach, Enslave, Manipulates And Creates A Breach To Operate

Many have fallen victim to the tricks and deception of the Satan. The Holy Spirit will help you to discern and disassociate yourself or any victim from any Satanic bondage.

1. **Obsession:** A persistent, disturbing, preoccupation with an unreasonable idea or feeling: a compelling or uncontrollable motivation.

2. **Depression:** An act of "depressing" or a state of being pressed down: a state of feeling down, sad, dejected, rejected, unwanted, unloved, or hunted. A psychoneurotic or psychotic disorder marked especially by sadness, inactivity, difficulty in thinking and concentration, a significant increase or decrease in appetite and time spent sleeping, feelings of dejection and hopelessness, and sometimes, suicidal tendencies.

3. **Possession:** To be possessed, taking into captivity: to take absolute control of. Control or occupancy of property without regard to ownership: Something owned, occupied, or controlled: dominated against ones will Example: a passion or an idea. A psychological or mental/emotional state in which an individual's normal personality or character is taken over or replaced by another force or entity. This can be by an evil spirit (demons), sex, drug or alcohol addiction, anger, bitterness, etc.

4. **Curse:** Pronouncement or Invocation for harm or injury to come upon someone: To call upon a supernatural power to send injury, curse or hurt upon someone. The evil that comes as if in response to imprecation or as retribution (Torment)

5. **Daily Satanic, Evil, Unbiblical Life Experience**: lust, immorality, sex before marriage, bitterness, anger, unforgiveness, hatred, low self-esteem, arrogance, pride, worldly music, bad company of friends etc.

6. **Unbelief,** Uncertainty, Doubt, Anger

7. **Confusion,** Inconsistency, Procrastination

8. **Poverty**, Failure, Sickness, Disease, Affliction etc.

From What Does One Need Deliverance & Healing

1. Any form of obsession, depression, possession, addiction, sin, curse, and soul ties, etc.

2. Chronic and bad attitude or behavior,

3. Uncontrollable lifestyles, drives, cravings, and appetite such as: smoking, alcohol, lying, compulsive anger, arrogance, unforgiveness, bitterness, money, paranoia, strife, hatred, filthy and impure thoughts, profanity, and pornography

4. Life Deception, low self-esteem, suicidal thoughts and wickedness, rebellion, insubordination

5. Satanism, chandelling, witchcraft, occult, cult, worship of nature and humans, psychic practices.

6. Undermining spirit (always seeing and saying evil things about others)

7. Sickness, disease, affliction, torment, Bad company of friends

8. Witchcraft Practices and Covens; Horoscope; Palm reading; Crystal ball; any organization that deals with the Occult, Cult, New Age Movement, etc.

9. Invocation and Communication with the dead, fallen angels, demons etc.

Biblical Examples Of Deliverance, Healing, Restoration

1. **Israel** Delivered from Egyptian Bondage
   The Book of Exodus

2. **God Delivers Israel** from Haman Through Queen Esther - The Book of Esther

3. **King David** Delivered from Life's Challenges
   Psalm 18; 35; 144:1-10

4. **King Saul** delivered from Demonic Possession **(Influence)** - I Samuel 16:17-23

5. **King Jehoshaphat** Delivered from Invasion
   2 Chron. 20

6. **The Four Leapers** and Israel delivered from hunger and degradation - 2 Kings 7

7. **The Deliverance And Healing Ministry Of Jesus Christ** - Isaiah 61:1-3; Luke 4:18-19; Matt. 4:23-25; Matt. 8:28-34; Matt. 12:15-21; Lk 4:40-41; 8:1-3; Mk. 13:10-19; John 9; Matt. 12:22-30

8. **The Deliverance & Healing Ministry Of the Early Apostles** - Acts 2:37-47; 3; 5:12-16; 8:4-25; 9:36-43; 19; Heb. 2:1-4 - The Whole Book Of Acts

9. **All Believers Are Commissioned to Preach, Teach God's Word; Cast Out Devils, Deliver** and Heal All Sickness, Diseases, Afflictions etc. Mk 3:13-15; Matt. 10:1-8; Matt. 24:18-20; Mk 16:15-20

Steps To Personal Deliverance, Healing, Restoration (The Same Steps Can Be Used To Set Others Free)

1. Identify the problem and face it boldly. Identify the root cause of the problem. If the situation cannot be probed, take it to prayer and ask the Holy Spirit to reveal the root cause. Make enquiries to verify if the problem is in your family line (ancestral/generational curse). Reject the belief and the thought that your situation is your destiny or God's plan for your life. John 10:10; 3 John 2

2. Take personal responsibility of the matter and stop blaming others. A higher percentage of all situations feeds on or operates by your emotions and will. That is, you could have avoided the situation by God's ability in you.

THE CHRISTIAN FOUNDATION

3. Forgive everyone who is involved in the situation or problem. You must forgive because Christ has forgiven you. Unforgiveness can hurt you. Matt. 6:9-15; Mark 11:23-26

4. Accept and believe that Jesus came to share His blood for your redemption (Deliverance and Healing). John 3:15-18; Acts 10; Hebrews 2:14-14; 4:14-16

5. Confess every known sin in your life and beyou are forgiven. Ps 51; I John 1:8-10. Accept God's forgiveness and forgive yourself. I John1:8-10

6. Most times, the intensity of the situation will demand a period of consecrated fast and prayer. Do not hesitate or procrastinate. Ecclesiastes 3; 9:11; John 9; Isa 58

7. Through the Blood of Jesus; the Name of Jesus; the authority of God's Word and your step of Faith, break every connection with every evil and sinful past and renounce them.

8. By God's authority invested in you, release yourself, or the victim, (walk in the spirit, Daily Devotional lifestyle of Prayer, Bible Study and Periodic Fasting.)

9. Make new friends with spiritually sound and matured Christians. Sometimes you may have to consult a matured and spirit-filled, consecrated Christian to help you.

10. Submit yourself to a True Bible believing and teaching Church or a Spirit-filled, sincere Pastor/Christian for proper Pastoral Care.

Biblical Foundation For Spiritual Growth & Maturity

11. Overcome all odds and share your faith with others. There will be times of temptation. Always remember God's Promise of protection, providence, healing, sound mind, guidance, etc. – Galatians 3, 5; James 1 – 5; Colossians; Ephesians; I and II Corinthians, etc.

12. Always depend on God's investment in you: The Name of Jesus; The Holy Spirit; The Word of God; Fasting and Prayer; Faith and Trust in God Word.

13. It is the will of God that you walk in health and prosperity even as your soul receives spiritual nourishment and prosperity.

STUDY LESSON VI
DELIVERANCE

In Your Own Words Define the following Words:

Curse _____

Depression_____

Obsession_____

Possession_____

Redemption_____

Blessing_____

Salvation_____

Healing _____

Deliverance_____

Who was Abraham? _____
_____

3. What was Abraham's connection to deliverance? _____
_____
_____

God: In Exodus 20:1-6, how is God described? _____
_____

Biblical Foundation For Spiritual Growth & Maturity

_____

_____

Gentiles: Who were the Gentiles? _____

_____

_____

_____

Key Scriptural References

Deliverance

1. What is bondage? _____

_____

2. What is deliverance? _____

_____

3. What does it mean to be cursed? _____

_____

_____

4. Briefly explain each of the following scriptures.

Exodus 20:3 _____

The Christian Foundation

Exodus 20:4-5 _____

_____

Exodus 20:7 _____

_____

Assurance

What is confession? _____

_____

What does cleanse us from all unrighteousness mean?

_____

_____

_____

Define condemnation. _____

_____

_____

_____

_____

Summarize I John 1:8-10 and Romans 8:1 into three statements of assurance

_____

_____

_____

_____

Deliverance

1. Pages 128, 129 and 130 define redemption. In your own words, expound on the following words:

Agorazo

_____

_____

_____

Exagorazo

_____

_____

_____

_____

_____

Lutro

_____

_____

_____

Apolutrosis

_____

_____

_____

2. Choose one example of the deliverance given above and expound on it

_____

_____

_____

_____

_____

_____

_____

_____

3. Self-Examination

List some of the many forms of bondages listed in this study

Basic Doctrines Of The Bible

II Timothy 3:16-17
*"All Scripture Is Given By Inspiration Of God,
And Is Profitable For Doctrine,
For Reproof, For Correction,
For Instruction In Righteousness:
That The Man Of God May Be Perfect,
Thoroughly Furnished Unto All Good Works."*

Chapter 7
Basic Doctrines Of The Bible

Biblical doctrine refers to the systematic and coherent study of the teachings and principles found in the Bible. Biblical Doctrine involves the humble and careful examination and interpretation of Scripture to understand God's character, nature, and plans for humanity.

***II Peter 1:16**-21 - "For we have not followed cunningly devised fables, when we made known unto you the power and coming of our Lord Jesus Christ, but were eyewitnesses of his majesty. For he received from God the Father honor and glory, when there came such a voice to him from the excellent glory, This is my beloved Son, in whom I am well pleased. And this voice which came from heaven we heard, when we were with him in the holy mount. We have also a more sure word of prophecy; whereunto ye do well that ye take heed, as unto a light that shineth in a dark place, until the day dawn, and the day star arise in your hearts:*

"Knowing this first, that no prophecy of the scripture is of any private interpretation. For the prophecy came not in old time by the will of man: but holy men of God spake as they were moved by the Holy Ghost.

II Timothy 3:16-17 *"All scripture is given by inspiration of God, and is profitable for doctrine, for reproof, for correction, for instruction in righteousness: That the man of God may be perfect, thoroughly furnished unto all good works."*

The Four Characteristics of Biblical Doctrine

1. **Spiritual Authority:** Biblical Doctrine is rooted in the authority of Scripture, recognizing the Bible as the inspired, infallible Word of God - II Tim. 3:16-17

2. **Systematic:** Biblical doctrine involves the systematic study of Scripture, considering the entire Biblical narrative, its various themes, motifs, and teachings.

3. **Coherent:** Biblical doctrine seeks to present a coherent and consistent understanding of God's character, nature, and plans, avoiding contradictions and paradoxes.

4. **Christ-Centered:** Biblical doctrine is Christ-Centered, recognizing Jesus Christ as the Central figure of Scripture and the ultimate revelation of God's character and nature - Hebrews 1:1-3.

Key Essential Doctrines of the Christian Faith

a. **The Triune God - (Elohim):** The doctrine of one God in three persons: Father, Son, and Holy Spirit - Matthew 28:19; 2 Corinthians 13:14

b. **The Deity of Christ:** The doctrine that Jesus Christ is fully God and fully human, the Son of God and the Savior of humanity (John 1:1-14; Hebrews 1:1-3).

c. **Salvation By Grace Through Faith In The Name Of Jesus:** The doctrine that salvation is a gift of God's grace, received through faith in Jesus Christ and His atoning work on the cross - Eph. 2:8-9; Rom. 3:24-25

d. **The Authority of Scripture**: The doctrine that the Bible is the inspired and infallible Word of God, the ultimate authority for faith and practice (2 Timothy 3:16-17; Psalm 119:160).

The Basic Foundational Doctrines Of The Bible Are:

1. God: That the one true God has revealed Himself as the eternally self-existent, self-revealed "I AM"; and has further revealed Himself as embodying the principles of relationship and association as Father, Son and Holy Ghost. *Deuteronomy 6:4; Mark 12:29; Isaiah 43:10-11; Matthew 28:19*

2. The Lord Jesus Christ: That the Deity of our Lord Jesus Christ, in His Virgin Birth, in His sinless life, in His miracles, in His vicarious death and atonement through His shed blood, in His bodily resurrection, in His ascension to the right hand of the Father, and in His personal and literal second coming in power and glory.

3. The Scriptures Inspired: That the Bible is the inspired Word of God, a revelation from God to men; the infallible rule of faith and conduct, and is superior to conscience and reason. (2 Timothy 3:15, 16; 1 Peter 2:2)

4. The Scriptures Inspired: That the unique divine inspiration of all canonical books of the Old and New Testaments as originally given, so that they are infallibly and uniquely authoritative and free from error of any sort, in all matters with which they deal, scientific and historical as well as moral and theological.

5. Special Creation: That the special creation of existing space-time universe and all its basic systems and kinds of organisms in the six literal days of the creation week.

6. The Genesis Curse & Origin Of Nations: That the full historicity and perspicuity of the Biblical record of primeval history, including the literal existence of Adam and Eve as the progenitors of all people, the literal fall and resultant divine curse on creation: world-wide cataclysmic deluge, and the origin of nations and languages at the tower of Babel.

7. Man: His Fall And Redemption: That man was created good and upright, for God said, *"Let us make man in Our image, after our likeness"*. But man, by voluntary transgression fell and his only hope of redemption is in Jesus Christ the Son of God. *Gen. 1:26-31; 3:1-7; Rom. 5:12-21*

8. Satan: That the existence of a personal, malignant being called Satan who acts as tempter and accuser, for whom the place of eternal punishment was prepared, where all who die outside of Christ shall be confined in conscious torment for eternity. *2 Corinthians 4:4; 1 Peter 5:8; Rev. 20:2*

9. The Salvation Of Man: That the Grace of God, which brings salvation hath appeared to all men, through the preaching of repentance toward God and faith toward the Lord Jesus Christ; Man is saved by the washing of regeneration and renewing of the Holy Ghost, and being justified by grace through faith, he becomes an heir of God according to the hope of eternal life. *Titus 2:11; Romans 10:13-15; Lk 24:47; Titus 3:5-7; 1 Jn 1:7-9; Heb. 9:13-28*

10. Water Baptism: That the ordinance of baptism by burial with Christ should be observed as commanded in the Scriptures, by all who have really repented and in their hearts have truly believed on Christ as Savior and Lord.

In so doing, they have the body washed in pure water as an outward symbol of cleansing, while their heart has already been sprinkled with the blood of Christ as an inner cleansing; thus they declare to the world that they have died with Jesus and that they have also been raised with Him to walk in newness of life. - *Matthew 28:19; Acts 10:47; Rom. 6:4; Acts 20:21; Heb. 10:22*

11. The Lord's Supper: That the Lord's Supper, consisting of the elements, bread and fruit of the vine, is the symbol expressing our sharing the divine nature of our Lord Jesus Christ. II Peter 1:4; a memorial of His suffering and death and a prophecy of His coming - 1 Corinthians 11:26); and is enjoined on all believers "until He comes." Feet washing: this is left to the discretion and option of the local church and pastor. - John 13:14: 1 Timothy 5:10

12. The Promise Of The Father: That all believers are entitled to, and should ardently expect, and earnestly seek, the promise of the Father, the Baptism in the Holy Ghost and fire; according to the command of the Lord Jesus Christ. This was the normal experience of all in the early Christian Church. With it, or subsequent to it, comes the enduement of power for life and service, the bestowment of the Gifts and their uses in the work of the ministry. (Luke 24:49; Acts 1:4; 1 Corinthians 12:1-31). This wonderful experience of the Baptism in the Holy Ghost is distinct from, and subsequent to the experience of the new birth. - *Acts 10:44-46; 11:14-16; 15:7-9*

13. The Evidence Of The Baptism In the Holy Ghost: That The believer's Baptism in the Holy Ghost is witnessed by the physical sign of speaking with other tongues as the Spirit of God gives them utterance (Acts 2:4). The speaking in tongues in this instance is the same in essence as the gift of tongues (1 Corinthians 12:4, 10, 28), but different in purpose and use.

14. Entire Sanctification: That the Scriptures teach a life of Holiness without which no man shall see the Lord. By the power of the Holy Ghost we are able to obey the command: Be Ye Holy, For I Am Holy." Entire sanctification is the will of God for all believers, and should be earnestly pursued by walking in obedience to God's Word. *Hebrews 12:14; 1 Peter 1:15-16, 1 Thess. 5:23-24; 1 John 2:6*

15. The Church: We believe the Church is the Body of Christ, the habitation of God through the Spirit, with divine appointments for the fulfillment of her great commission. Each believer, born of the spirit, is an integral part of the General Assembly and Church of the First-Born, which are written in heaven. *Ephe. 1:22-23; 2:22; Hebrews 12:23*

16. The Ministry & Evangelism: We believe that a divinely called and scripturally ordained ministry has been provided by our Lord for a two-fold purpose: (A) The evangelization of the world, and (B) The edifying of the Body of Christ. *Mark 16:15-20; Ephesians 4:11-13*

17. Divine Healing: We believe that deliverance from sickness is provided for in the atonement, and is the privilege of all believers. *Isaiah 53:4-5; Matthew 8:16-17*
18. The Second Coming Of Christ: That the resurrection

of those who have fallen asleep in Christ and their translation, together with those who are alive and remain unto the coming of the Lord, is the blessed hope of the Church. *1 Thess. 4:16-18; Rom. 8:23; Titus 2:13 1 Cor. 15:51-52; Rev. 11:15*

19. The Millennial Reign Of Jesus Christ: We believe that the revelation of the Lord Jesus Christ from heaven, the salvation of national Israel, and the millennial reign of Christ on the earth is the scriptural promise and the world's hope. *2 Thessalonians 1:7-10; Revelation 19:11-14; Romans 11:26-27; Rev. 20:1-7*

20. The Lake Of fire: We believe that the devil and his angels, the Beast and the false prophet, and whosoever is not found written in the Book of Life, shall be consigned to everlasting punishment in the lake which burns with fire and brimstone, which is the second death. *Rev. 19:20; 20:10-15*

21. The New Heavens And the New Earth: We, "according to His promise look for new heaven and new earth wherein dwells righteousness." *2 Peter 2:13; Revelation 21:22*

The Doctrine Of Angels

Psalm 103:19-22

"The LORD hath prepared his throne in the heavens; and his kingdom ruleth over all.

"Bless the LORD, ye his angels, that excel in strength, that do his commandments, hearkening unto the voice of his word. Bless ye the LORD, all ye his hosts; ye ministers of his, that do his pleasure. Bless the LORD, all his works in all places of his dominion: bless the LORD, O my soul."

Chapter 8
Angels

The Supremacy of Christ Jesus Over Angels & All Spiritual Beings & Entities - (Hebrews 1:1-7, 13,14) *"God, who at sundry times and in divers manners spoke in time past unto the fathers by the prophets, Hath in these last days spoken unto us by his Son, whom he hath appointed heir of all things, by whom also he made the world: Who being the brightness of his glory, and the express image of his person, and upholding all things by the word of his power, when he had by himself purged our sins, sat down on the right hand of the Majesty on high; Being made so much better than the angels, as he hath by inheritance obtained a more excellent name than they.*

"For unto which of the angels said he at any time, Thou art my Son, this day have I begotten thee? And again, I will be to him a Father, and he shall be to me a Son? And again, when he bringeth in the first begotten into the world, he saith, And let all the angels of God worship him. And of the angels he saith, Who maketh his angels spirits, and his ministers a flame of fire. But unto the Son he saith, Thy throne, O God, is for ever and ever: a sceptre of righteousness is the sceptre of thy kingdom. **But to which of the angels said he at any time, Sit on my right hand, until I make thine enemies thy footstool?** *Are they not all ministering spirits, sent forth to minister for them who shall be heirs of salvation?"*

Colossians 1:14-20 *"In whom (In Christ Jesus) we have redemption through his blood, even the forgiveness of sins: Who is the image of the invisible God, the firstborn of every creature:*

"For by him were all things created, that are in heaven, and that are in earth, visible and invisible, whether they be thrones, or dominions, or principalities, or powers: all things were created by him, and for him: And he is before all things, and by him all things consist: And he is the head of the body, the church: who is the beginning, the firstborn from the dead; that in all things he might have the preeminence. For it pleased the Father that in him should all fulness dwell; And, having made peace through the blood of his cross, by him to reconcile all things unto himself; by him, I say, whether they be things in earth, or things in heaven."

The Origins & Definitions Of Angels

1. Angels Are Created Beings - Angels were created by God. The time of their creation is not definitely specified. There is the strong possibility that God created the angels immediately after He had created the heavens and before He created the earth.

Genesis 1:1 "In the beginning God created the heavens and the earth."

Job 38:4-7 "The sons of God shouted for joy" when He laid the foundations of the earth."

Nehemiah 9:6 "Thou, even thou, art LORD alone; thou hast made heaven, the heaven of heavens, with all their host, the earth, and all things that are therein, the seas, and all that is therein, and thou preservest them all; and the host of heaven worshippeth thee."

John 1:1-5 "In the beginning was the Word, and the Word was with God, and the Word was God. The same was in the beginning with God. All things were made by him; and without him was not anything made that was made. In him was life; and the life was the light of men. And the light shineth in darkness; and the darkness comprehended it not."

2. Angels And Other Heavenly Bodies Were Created – In Psalm 148 The Psalmist Calls Upon All In The Celestial Heavens, Including The Angels, To Praise God.

The Reason Given Is: (Psalm 148)

"For He Commanded, And They Were Created. Praise ye the LORD from the heavens: praise him in the heights. Praise ye him, all his angels: praise ye him, all his hosts. Praise ye him, sun and moon: praise him, all ye stars of light. Praise him, ye heavens of heavens and ye waters that be above the heavens. Let them praise the name of the LORD: for he commanded, and they were created. He hath also stablished them forever and ever: he hath made a decree which shall not pass.

"Praise the LORD from the earth, ye dragons, and all deeps: Fire, and hail; snow, and vapor; stormy wind fulfilling his word: Mountains, and all hills; fruitful trees, and all cedars: Beasts, and all cattle; creeping things, and flying fowl: Kings of the earth, and all people; princes, and all judges of the earth: Both young men, and maidens; old men, and children:

"Let them praise the name of the LORD: for his name alone is excellent; his glory is above the earth and heaven.

"He also exalteth the horn of his people, the praise of all his saints; even of the children of Israel, a people near unto him. Praise ye the LORD"

3. Christ Jesus Is God, Not A Created Angel. Christ Jesus is God's Word Incarnate: The Word of God Becoming Flesh. He is God. God Created all things by His Word - JESUS.

All Creation came into existence by the Word of God: including angels. Christ Jesus is the Word of God Incarnate. Jesus created all things. Jesus is the Creator. Jesus is Lord Over all Angels and all Creation. Jesus was not created. Lucifer and all angels were created and are created beings. Jesus is God's Word Incarnate.

4. God is One. He manifests Himself in three Persons yet one. Jesus Christ is the Second Manifestation of the Triune God (One God – Jehovah, who Manifests Himself in Three Ways – Father, Son and The Holy Spirit).

5. Jesus Is The Direct Image Of The Invisible God. He is God. - *Genesis 1:1-3 "In the beginning God created the heavens and the earth."*

6. He is God's Word Incarnate. By Him All Things Were Created. *John 1:1-5; 11-14 "In the beginning was the Word, and the Word was with God, and the Word was God. The same was in the beginning with God. All things were made by him; and without him was not anything made that was made. In him was life; and the life was the light of men. And the light shineth in darkness; and the darkness comprehended it not.*

"He came unto his own, and his own received him not. But as many as received him, to them gave he power to become the sons of God, even to them that believe on his name: Which were born, not of blood, nor of the will of the flesh, nor of the will of man, but of God. And the Word was made flesh, and dwelt among us, (and we beheld his glory, the glory as of the only begotten of the Father,) full of grace and truth."

1Timothy 3:16 "And without controversy great is the mystery of godliness: God was manifest in the flesh, justified in the Spirit, seen of angels, preached unto the Gentiles, believed on in the world, received up into glory."

Colossians 1:15,16 "Who (Jesus) is the image of the invisible God, the firstborn of every creature: For by him were all things created, that are in heaven, and that are in earth, visible and invisible, whether they be thrones, or dominions, or principalities, or powers: all things were created by him, and for him: And he is before all things, and by him all things consist."

The Host Of Heaven Worship Jesus Not Angels

Revelation 5:6-14 "And I beheld, and, lo, in the midst of the throne and of the four beasts, and in the midst of the elders, stood a Lamb as it had been slain, having seven horns and seven eyes, which are the seven Spirits of God sent forth into all the earth. And he came and took the book out of the right hand of him that sat upon the throne. And when he had taken the book, the four beasts and four and twenty elders fell down before the Lamb, having every one of them harps, and golden vials full of odours, which are the prayers of saints.

"And they sung a new song, saying, thou art worthy to take the book, and to open the seals thereof: for thou wast slain, and hast redeemed us to God by thy blood out of every kindred, and tongue, and people, and nation; And hast made us unto our God kings and priests: and we shall reign on the earth. And I beheld, and I heard the voice of many angels round about the throne and the beasts and the elders: and the number of them was ten thousand times ten thousand, and thousands of thousands; Saying with a loud voice, Worthy is the Lamb that was slain to receive power, and riches, and wisdom, and strength, and honor, and glory, and blessing. And every creature which is in heaven, and on the earth, and under the earth, and such as are in the sea, and all that are in them, heard I saying: Blessing, and honour, and glory, and power, be unto him that sitteth upon the throne, and unto the Lamb forever and ever. And the four beasts said, Amen. And the four and twenty elders fell down and worshipped him that liveth forever and ever."

When Did God Create Angels

The time of the Creation of Angels is never stated. However, we know they were created before the creation of the world. From the book of Job, we are told they were present when the earth was created:

Job 38:4-8 "Gird up now thy loins like a man; for I will demand of thee and answer thou me. Where wast thou when I laid the foundations of the earth? Declare, if thou hast understanding. Who hath laid the measures thereof, if thou knowest? Or who hath stretched the line upon it? Whereupon are the foundations thereof fastened?

"Or who laid the corner stone thereof: "*When the morning stars sang together, and all the sons of God shouted for joy? Or who shut up the sea with doors, when it broke forth, as if it had issued out of the womb?"*

The Nature Of Their Creation

1. **Angels Are Created Beings** – They were created simultaneously as a company, a countless host of myriads - *Colossians 1:16 "For by him (Christ Jesus) were all things created, that are in heaven, and that are in earth, visible and invisible, whether they be thrones, or dominions, or principalities, or powers: all things were created by him, and for him:"*

   Nehemiah 9:6 "Thou, even thou, art LORD alone; thou hast made heaven, the heaven of heavens, with all their host, the earth, and all things that are therein, the seas, and all that is therein, and thou preservest them all; and the host of heaven worshippeth thee."

2. **Angels Are Spirit Beings** - Though Angels are known to have the ability to sometimes appear in human form as in Genesis 18:3; They are described as "spirits" or spirit beings: *Hebrews 1:14 "Are they not all ministering spirits, sent forth to minister for them who shall be heirs of salvation?"*

3. **Angels Do Not Have Material Bodies As We Do** - Angels do not function as human beings nor are they subject to death.

Mark 12:25 "For when they shall rise from the dead, they neither marry, nor are given in marriage; but are as the angels which are in heaven.

Luke 20:34b-36 "The children of this world marry and are given in marriage: But they which shall be accounted worthy to obtain that world, and the resurrection from the dead, neither marry, nor are given in marriage: Neither can they die any more: for they are equal unto the angels; and are the children of God, being the children of the resurrection."

4. **Angels Are Not Created In God's Image** - They do not share man's glorious destiny of redemption in Christ. At the consummation of the age, the redeemed will judge angels. - *1 Corinthians 6:3 "Know ye not that we shall judge angels? How much more things that pertain to this life?"*

5. **Angels Are Not Omnipresent** - They cannot be everywhere at once.

6. **Angels Are Not To Be Worshipped** – They are not to be classified as "God" or Gods.

Isaiah 42:5, 8, 10-13 "Thus, saith God the LORD, he that created the heavens, and stretched them out; he that spread forth the earth, and that which cometh out of it; He that giveth breath unto the people upon it, and spirit to them that walk therein: I am the LORD: that is my name: and my glory will I not give to another, neither my praise to graven images. Sing unto the LORD a new song and his praise from the end of the earth, ye that go down to the sea, and all that is therein, the isles, and the inhabitants thereof. Let the wilderness and the cities thereof lift up their voice, the villages that Kedar doth inhabit: Let the inhabitants of the rock sing, let them shout from the top of the mountains.

"Let them give glory unto the LORD and declare his praise in the islands. The LORD shall go forth as a mighty man, he shall stir up jealousy like a man of war: he shall cry, yea, roar; he shall prevail against his enemies.

Revelation 22:8-9 "And I John saw these things and heard them: And when I had heard and seen, I fell down to worship before the feet of the angel which shewed me these things: Then saith he unto me, see thou do it not: for I am thy fellow-servant, and of thy brethren the prophets and of them which keep the sayings of this book: worship God."

7. **Angels Are Subject To Authority** - Like all creation, angels are under God's authority and are subject to His Order and judgment

   I Corinthians 6:3 "Know ye not that we shall judge angels? how much more things that pertain to this life?

   "If then ye have judgments of things pertaining to this life, set them to judge who are least esteemed in the Church."

   Matthew 25:41 "Then shall he say also unto them on the left hand, depart from me, ye cursed, into everlasting fire, prepared for the devil and his angels"

Definition Of Angel

The Word "ANGEL" (ANGELOS): Means "Messenger" (From Angello "To Deliver A Message): Sent: whether by God, Man or Satan. Angels are spirit beings and have no material bodies as men. Angels can reveal themselves in human form.

Hebrews 1:5-7 "For unto which of the angels said he at any time: Thou art my Son, this day have I begotten thee? And again, I will be to him a Father, and he shall be to me a Son? And again, when he bringeth in the first begotten into the world, he saith: And let all the angels of God worship him. And of the angels he saith, Who maketh his angels spirits, and his ministers a flame of fire."

Luke 1:11-17 "And there appeared unto him an angel of the Lord standing on the right side of the altar of incense. And when Zacharias saw him, he was troubled, and fear fell upon him. But the angel said unto him, Fear not, Zacharias: for thy prayer is heard; and thy wife Elisabeth shall bear thee a son, and thou shalt call his name John. And thou shalt have joy and gladness; and many shall rejoice at his birth.

Luke 24:4,23 "And it came to pass, as they were much perplexed thereabout, behold, two men stood by them in shining garments: And as they were afraid, and bowed down their faces to the earth, they said unto them: Why seek ye the living among the dead? He is not here but is risen, remember how he spake unto you when he was yet in Galilee... And when they found not his body, they came, saying, that they had also seen a vision of angels, which said that he was alive."

Acts 10:3,30 "He saw in a vision evidently about the ninth hour of the day an angel of God coming in to him, and saying unto him, Cornelius... And Cornelius said, four days ago I was fasting until this hour; and at the ninth hour I prayed in my house, and behold, a man stood before me in bright clothing."

The Word "Angel" is also used of "Guardian" or "Representative"

Revelation 1:20 "...The seven stars are the angels of the seven Churches: and the seven candlesticks which thou sawest are the seven Churches."

Matthew 18:10 "Take heed that ye despise not one of these little ones; for I say unto you, that in heaven their angels do always behold the face of my Father which is in heaven."

Acts 12:15 "And they said unto her, Thou art mad. But she constantly affirmed that it was even so. Then said they, It is his angel."

Types, Classes And Ranks Of Angels

There are different types, classes, and ranks of Angels. There are three different Words used for other ranks of beings, whereas the primary word used in the Bible to describe all of them is Angel. The other three are: Seraphim, Cherubim and Ministering Spirits.

Seraphim – Isaiah 6:1-4 - *"In the year that king Uzziah died I saw also the Lord sitting upon a throne, high and lifted up, and his train filled the temple.*

*"Above it stood the **Seraphim**: each one had six wings; with twain he covered his face, and with twain he covered his feet, and with twain he did fly.*

"And one cried unto another, and said, Holy, holy, holy, is the LORD of hosts: the whole earth is full of his glory.

"And the posts of the door moved at the voice of him that cried, and the house was filled with smoke."

Cherubim - Ezekiel 10:1-3 - *"Then I looked, and behold, in the firmament that was above the head of the **Cherubim** there appeared over them as it were a sapphire stone, as the appearance of the likeness of a throne. And he spake unto the man clothed with linen, and said, go in between the wheels, even under the cherub, and fill thine hand with coals of fire from between the **Cherubim**, and scatter them over the city. And he went in in my sight. Now the **Cherubim** stood on the right side of the house, when the man went in; and the cloud filled the inner court."*

Ministering Spirits, which is more of a description than name: *Hebrews 1:13, 12* – *"But to which of the angels said he at any time, Sit on my right hand, until I make thine enemies thy footstool? Are they not all ministering spirits, sent forth to minister for them who shall be heirs of salvation?"*

The Hebrew Word For Angel Is Mal`Ach, And The Greek Word Is Angelos - Both words mean "messenger" and describes one who executes the purpose and will of the one whom they serve. There are two main categories of angels.

The First is the Elect, Good, Holy Or Unfallen Angels.

The holy angels are messengers of God, serving Him and doing His Will.

The Second Group is the Evil or Fallen Angels.
The fallen angels serve Satan, the god of this world (aiwn, "age"):

II Corinthians 4:3, 4 - "But if our gospel be hiding, it is hiding to them that are lost: In whom the god of this world hath blinded the minds of them which believe not, lest the light of the glorious gospel of Christ, who is the image of God, should shine unto them."

The Nine Celestial Orders Of Angels

Many have suggested that there are nine celestial orders of Angels, Choirs or Hierarchy.

When angels are mentioned in Scripture, generally it is the class of holy angels in view.

By contrast, the fallen angels are those who have not maintained their holiness and holy habitation.

In each group the angels are in different classes, ranks and responsibilities.

Some of the angels are either named and classified or described in scripture.

Suggested Celestial Order Of Angels:

First Sphere
- Seraphim
- Cherubim
- Thrones

Second Sphere
    a. Dominions or Lordships
    b. Virtues or Strongholds
    c. Powers or Authorities

Third Sphere
    d. Principalities or Rulers
    e. Archangels
    f. Angels
    g. Personal Guardian Angels

Seraphim

Seraphim (Singular: **Seraph**. Plural: **Seraphim**): Meaning "Burning Ones" Or Nobles

The Seraphim are mentioned only once in Scripture. The Seraphim are the highest order of angels. They serve as the caretakers of God's Throne and continuously singing his praises. They surround the throne of God singing the music of the spheres and regulating the movement of the heavens as it emanates from God.

These beings apparently served as agents of purification for Isaiah, as he began his prophetic ministry. When he received a revelation on the purity of God, he also saw his own filthiness and unworthiness.

Unlike the New Testament, Isaiah did not have the privilege of the Blood of Jesus. A Seraphim flew with live coal in his hand, which he had taken with tongs from the altar. He laid it upon his mouth, and said: *"Lo, this hath touched thy lips; and thine iniquity is taken away, and thy sin purged."*

Isaiah 6:1-7 "In the year that king Uzziah died I saw also the Lord sitting upon a throne, high and lifted up, and his train filled the temple. Above it stood the Seraphims: each one had six wings; with twain he covered his face, and with twain he covered his feet, and with twain he did fly. And one cried unto another, and said, Holy, holy, holy, is the LORD of hosts: the whole earth is full of his glory. And the posts of the door moved at the voice of him that cried, and the house was filled with smoke. Then said I, Woe is me! For I am undone; because I am a man of unclean lips, and I dwell in the midst of a people of unclean lips: for mine eyes have seen the King, the LORD of hosts. Then flew one of the Seraphims unto me, having a live coal in his hand, which he had taken with the tongs from off the altar: And he laid it upon my mouth, and said, Lo, this hath touched thy lips; and thine iniquity is taken away, and thy sin purged."

Cherubim

Singular: **Cherub**. Plural: **Cherubim** or Cherubs

They are living creatures who defend God's Holiness. The Cherubim are first mentioned in the Bible in Genesis 3:24: *"After He drove the man out, He placed on the east side of the Garden of Eden* **Cherubim And A Flaming Sword** *flashing back and forth to guard the way to the tree of life."*

The Cherubim are symbolic of God's holy presence and his majesty. The Cherubim Occupy a unique position. Moses Makes Mercy Seat With Cherubim Overlooking It:

Exodus 25:17-22; "And thou shalt make a mercy seat of pure gold: two cubits and a half shall be the length thereof, and a cubit and a half the breadth thereof. And thou shalt make two **Cherubim Of Gold***, of beaten work shalt thou make them, in the two ends of the mercy seat. And make one Cherub on the one end, and the other Cherub on the other end: even of the mercy seat shall ye make the Cherubim on the two ends thereof.*

"And the Cherubim shall stretch forth their wings on high, covering the mercy seat with their wings, and their faces shall look one to another; toward the mercy seat shall the faces of the Cherubim be.

"And thou shalt put the mercy seat above upon the ark; and in the ark thou shalt put the testimony that I shall give thee. And there I will meet with thee, and I will commune with thee from above the mercy seat, from between the two Cherubim which are upon the ark of the testimony, of all things which I will give thee in commandment unto the children of Israel."

Exodus 26:1 "Moreover thou shalt make the tabernacle with ten curtains of fine twined linen, and blue, and purple, and scarlet: with Cherubim of cunning work shalt thou make them.

Cherubim Described By Ezekiel In The Chapters 1 And 10 Of The Book Of Ezekiel As The Four Living Creatures - Ezekiel 1:5

a. **Each Has Four Faces** - that of a man, a lion, an ox, and an eagle - Ezekiel 1:10; 10:14. In their appearance, they have the likeness of a man" - Ezekiel 1:5

b. **Each Has Four Wings** - They use two of their wings for flying and the other two for covering their bodies - Ezekiel 1:6, 11, 23

c. **Under Their Wings** - The Cherubim Appears To Have The Form, Likeness, of a Man's Hand - Ezekiel 1:8; 10:7-8, 21).

The Cherubim Serves The Purpose Of Magnifying The Holiness And Power Of God - Revelation 4:6-9 - This is one of their main responsibilities throughout the Bible.

a. **They Worship and Sings God's Praise.** They also serve as a visible reminder of the majesty and glory of God and His abiding presence with His people.

b. **Before Lucifer Fell He was an anointed Cherub:** Ezekiel 28:12-15 - *"Son of man take up a lamentation upon the king of Tyrus, and say unto him, Thus saith the Lord GOD; Thou sealest up the sum, full of wisdom, and perfect in beauty. Thou hast been in Eden the garden of God; every precious stone was thy covering, the sardius, topaz, and the diamond, the beryl, the onyx, and the jasper, the sapphire, the emerald, and the carbuncle, and gold: the workmanship of thy tabrets and of thy pipes was prepared in thee in the day that* *thou wast created. Thou art the anointed cherub that covereth; and I have set thee so: thou wast upon the holy mountain of God; thou hast walked up and down in the midst of the stones of fire. Thou wast perfect in thy ways from the day that thou wast created, till iniquity was found in thee."*

The Archangels

The word archangel is used only twice in the canonical Scripture but several times in the Septuagint, once to refer to Michael the archangel. Gabriel and Michael are the only two archangels named in the New Testament of the Bible.

Archangel Michael

Michael means: "Who is like God" He appears to be responsible for defense in the affairs of Israel and God's People in general. The Book of Daniel gives us a fascinating glimpse into the order, activities, and warfare of the Angels in the heavens and the earth – the celestial and terrestrial worlds. Daniel sets himself to fast and pray for Israel's freedom from captivity. The enormity of Gabriel's message assigned as response to Daniel's prayer provokes the demonic territorial Angel – the Prince of Persia (in charge of the Persian Kingdom that ruled the then World) to contend and resist Gabriel. The battle went on until Michael (the Warring Angel of Israel) was summoned to assist.

Daniel 10: 12, 13, 21; Daniel 12:1 "Then said he unto me, Fear not, Daniel: for from the first day that thou didst set thine heart to understand and to chasten thyself before thy God, thy words were heard, and I am come for thy words.

But the prince of the kingdom of Persia withstood me one and twenty days: but, lo, Michael, one of the chief princes, came to help me; and I remained there with the kings of Persia. But I will shew thee that which is noted in the scripture of truth: there is none that holdeth with me in these things, but Michael your prince."

Jude 1:9 "Yet Michael the archangel, when contending with the devil he disputed about the body of Moses, durst not bring against him a railing accusation, but said, The Lord rebuke thee." Revelation 12:7 "And there was war in heaven: Michael and his angels fought against the dragon; and the dragon fought and his angels."
Archangel Gabriel

The name Gabriel means: "Hero of God" or "God is Strong" – The Archangel Gabriel appears to be in charge of special communications. This is obvious in each of the four times he appears in the Bible: Gabriel reveals important message to Daniel after his 21 Days of fasting and Prayer:
- Israel's release from captivity
- The destinies of nations of the world
- The establishment of Jerusalem
- The coming Messiah
- The coming son of perdition (anti-Christ)
- The tribulation and desecration of the temple
- The consummation, etc.

In the New Testament Archangel Gabriel announces:
- The birth of John the Baptist to Zacharias – Lk. 1
- The birth of Jesus to Mary and Joseph –Luke 1, 2

The Watchers

The word "Watchers" comes out of Aramaic, meaning "Holy One" - It denotes vigilance, waking or watchful. In the Book of Daniel, the Watchers are depicted to be obedient angels, but in other references they are referred to as fallen angels.

The term "holy one" was used by Nebuchadnezzar when he saw a Watcher from heaven. This describes holy angels who are constantly vigilant to serve the Lord and who watch over the rulers of the world in the affairs of humanity

"This matter is by the decree of the watchers, and the demand by the word of the holy ones" in order that *"the living may know that the Most High rules in the kingdom of men..." Daniel 4:13, 17, 23-37.*

The phrase "Holy One" definitely implies there are unholy watchers - evil entities, who are also watching the affairs of men and seeking to influence or even destroy. There are innumerable angels in the creation of God.

Biblical Record Of Angelic Activities

Angels On Assignment At The Throne Of God
1. They are attendants around His throne, waiting on and serving Him and doing God's bidding -Ps. 103:20; Isa. 6; Job 1:6; 2:1; Rev. 5:11; 8
2. As Worshippers In Praise Of God - Isa. 6:3; Ps. 148: 1-2; Heb. 1:6; Rev. 5:12
3. As Observers Who Rejoice Over What God Does - Job 38: 6-7; Luke 2:12-13; 15:10

Angelic Assignment To Jesus:

1. His birth - Matt. 1:20; Luke 1:26-28; 2:8-15
2. An angel warned Joseph to take Mary and the baby Jesus and flee into Egypt. An angel directed the family to return to Israel after Herod died.
3. Angels ministered to Jesus in the wilderness Matt. 4:11
4. Angels ministered to Jesus In His stress in the Garden of Gethsemane - Luke 22:43 - He could have called a legion of angels to come to His defense. Matt. 26:53
5. At the resurrection of Jesus - an angel rolled away the stone from the tomb Matthew 28:1-2
6. Angels announced Jesus' resurrection to the women Matthew 285-6; Luke 24:5-7
7. Angels appeared after Jesus' ascension to comfort the disciples and announce His 2nd coming Acts 1:10-11
8. In relation to His coming again, the voice of the archangel will be heard at the translation of the Church -1 Thess. 4:16
9. Angels will accompany Jesus in His Glorious Second Coming to Earth - Matthew 25:31; 2 Thess. 1:7
10. Angels will enforce God's judgment at the end - Gen. 19:13; Rev. 14:6-7; Acts 12:23; Rev 16:1
11. Angels will separate (the wheat from the tares) the righteous from the unrighteous at the last judgment Matthew 13:39-40

Angelic Assignment To God's People And The Church

1. **They Minister to Heirs of Salvation** *"Are they not all ministering spirits, sent forth to minister for them who shall be heirs of salvation?*

The Christian Foundation

2. **Guarded By Special Angels** - *II Kings 6:17 - "And Elisha prayed, and said, LORD, I pray thee, open his eyes that he may see. And the LORD opened the eyes of the young man; and he saw: and, behold, the mountain was full of horses and chariots of fire round about Elisha. Psalm 91:10-13 - "There shall no evil befall thee, neither shall any plague come nigh thy dwelling. For he shall give his angels charge over thee to keep thee in all thy ways: They shall bear thee up in their hands, lest thou dash thy foot against a stone."*

3. **Guard and Guide Out Of Trouble** - Angels delivered Lot and his family from Sodom and Gomorrah – Genesis 18, 19

4. **Ministered to Jacob** – He saw a host of God's angels ascending and descending a ladder between him and the throne of God. Gen. 28

5. **They Help In Bringing People To The Savior** - Acts 8:26; 10:3; They minister, defend, direct course and encourage in times of danger - Acts 27:23-24; Acts 10

6. **They Minister To The Soul Of The Departed** – *"And it came to pass, that the beggar died, and was carried by the angels into Abraham's bosom: the rich man also died, and was buried Luke 16:22*

7. **Assigned By God To Give Protection To The Elect** – *"And then shall he send his angels, and shall gather together his elect from the four winds, from the uttermost part of the earth to the uttermost part of heaven." Mark 13:27*

8. **Special Angels Minister To Children** - *"Take heed that ye despise not one of these little ones; for I say unto you, that in heaven their angels do always behold the face of my Father which is in heaven." Matthew 18:10.*

9. **Angels Minister to Nations:** – Zechariah 6; Rev. 1-22.

10. **They Watch Over, Strengthen And Influence Rulers And Nations.** Michael, the archangel serving Israel - Daniel 10:13, 21; 12:1; Jude 9. In the Tribulation they will be the agents God uses to pour out His Judgments Revelation 8-9 and 16

God Uses Fallen Angels For His Purpose

"He cast upon them the fierceness of his anger, wrath, and indignation, and trouble, by sending evil angels among them." Psalm 78:49

Saul Was Tormented - *I Samuel 16:14-16 – "Then Samuel took the horn of oil, and anointed him in the midst of his brethren: and the Spirit of the LORD came upon David from that day forward. So Samuel rose up, and went to Ramah. But the Spirit of the LORD departed from Saul, and an evil spirit from the LORD troubled him. And Saul's servants said unto him, Behold now, an evil spirit from God troubleth thee. Let our lord now command thy servants, which are before thee, to seek out a man, who is a cunning player on an harp: and it shall come to pass, when the evil spirit from God is upon thee, that he shall play with his hand, and thou shalt be well. And Saul said unto his servants, Provide me now a man that can play well, and bring him to me.*

1 Samuel 18:10,11 - *"And it came to pass on the morrow, that the evil spirit from God came upon Saul, and he prophesied in the midst of the house: and David played with his hand, as at other times: and there was a javelin in Saul's hand. And Saul cast the javelin; for he said, I will smite David even to the wall with it. And David avoided out of his presence twice."*

Ahab Was Deceived - *1 Kings 22:19-23* - *"And he said, hear thou therefore the word of the LORD: I saw the LORD sitting on his throne, and all the host of heaven standing by him on his right hand and on his left. And the LORD said, who shall persuade Ahab that he may go up and fall at Ramothgilead? And one said on this manner, and another said on that manner. And there came forth a spirit, and stood before the LORD, and said, I will persuade him.*

"And the LORD said unto him, wherewith? And he said, I will go forth, and I will be a lying spirit in the mouth of all his prophets. And he said, thou shalt persuade him, and prevail also: go forth, and do so. Now therefore, behold, the LORD hath put a lying spirit in the mouth of all these thy prophets, and the LORD hath spoken evil concerning thee."

Angels Are Guardians Of The Gates Of The New Eternal City

Revelation 21:9-13 - *"And there came unto me one of the seven angels which had the seven vials full of the seven last plagues, and talked with me, saying, come hither, I will shew thee the bride, the Lamb's wife. And he carried me away in the spirit to a great and high mountain, and shewed me that great city, the holy Jerusalem, descending out of heaven from God, Having the glory of God: and her light was like unto a stone most precious, even like a jasper stone, clear as crystal; And had a wall great and high, and had twelve gates, and at the gates twelve angels, and names written thereon, which are the names of the twelve tribes of the children of Israel: On the east three gates; on the north three gates; on the south three gates; and on the west three gates."*

Angels Minister To The Heirs Of Salvation
"Are they not all ministering spirits, sent forth to minister for them who shall be heirs of salvation?" Hebrews 1:14

Angels Rejoice When Sinners Repent - Luke 15:7-10

Angels Minister To Little Ones - Matthew 18:10

Agents Of God's Providence For All Believers
- The Early Church - Acts of the Apostles
- Paul's journey to Rome – Acts 9-28
- In the affairs of nations – Daniel and Revelation
- Companions and guardians in daily life's journeys

Psalm 91:9-13 - *"Because thou hast made the LORD, which is my refuge, even the Most High, thy habitation; there shall no evil befall thee, neither shall any plague come nigh thy dwelling.*

"For he shall give his angels charge over thee to keep thee in all thy ways; they shall bear thee up in their hands, lest thou dash thy foot against a stone. Thou shalt tread upon the lion and adder: the young lion and the dragon shalt thou trample under feet."

Beware Of Fallen Angels And Demons Propagating False Doctrines And Sometimes Go Undercover As Angels Of Light - Deception

1 Timothy 4:1 -5 *"Now the Spirit speaketh expressly, that in the latter times some shall depart from the faith, giving heed to seducing spirits, and doctrines of devils; Speaking lies in hypocrisy; having their conscience seared with a hot iron; Forbidding to marry, and commanding to abstain from meats, which God hath created to be received with thanksgiving of them which believe and know the truth. For every creature of God is good, and nothing to be refused, if it be received with thanksgiving: For it is sanctified by the word of God and prayer"*

Jude 1:1-25 *"Jude, the servant of Jesus Christ, and brother of James, to them that are sanctified by God the Father, and preserved in Jesus Christ, and called: Mercy unto you, and peace, and love, be multiplied.*

"Beloved, when I gave all diligence to write unto you of the common salvation, it was needful for me to write unto you, and exhort you that ye should earnestly contend for the faith which was once delivered unto the saints.

"For there are certain men crept in unawares, who were before of old ordained to this condemnation, ungodly men, turning the grace of our God into lasciviousness, and denying the only Lord God, and our Lord Jesus Christ.

" I will therefore put you in remembrance, though ye once knew this, how that the Lord, having saved the people out of the land of Egypt, afterward destroyed them that believed not.

"And the angels which kept not their first estate, but left their own habitation, he hath reserved in everlasting chains under darkness unto the judgment of the great day.

"Even as Sodom and Gomorrha, and the cities about them in like manner, giving themselves over to fornication, and going after strange flesh, are set forth for an example, suffering the vengeance of eternal fire. Likewise, also these filthy dreamers defile the flesh.

"Yet Michael the archangel, when contending with the devil he disputed about the body of Moses, durst not bring against him a railing accusation, but said, The Lord rebuke thee. But these speak evil of those things which they know not: but what they know naturally, as brute beasts, in those things they corrupt themselves.

"Woe unto them! For they have gone in the way of Cain and ran greedily after the error of Balaam for reward and perished in the gainsaying of Core. These are spots in your feasts of charity, when they feast with you, feeding themselves without fear: clouds they are without water, carried about of winds; trees whose fruit withered, without fruit, twice dead, plucked up by the roots; Raging waves of the sea, foaming out their own shame; wandering stars, to whom is reserved the blackness of darkness forever.

"And Enoch also, the seventh from Adam, prophesied of these, saying, Behold, the Lord cometh with ten thousands of his saints, To execute judgment upon all, and to convince all that are ungodly among them of all their ungodly deeds which they have ungodly committed, and of all their hard speeches which ungodly sinners have spoken against him.

"These are murmurers, complainers, walking after their own lusts; and their mouth speaketh great swelling words, having men's persons in admiration because of advantage. But, beloved, remember ye the words which were spoken before of the apostles of our Lord Jesus Christ; How that they told you there should be mockers in the last time, who should walk after their own ungodly lusts. These be they who separate themselves, sensual, having not the Spirit. But ye, beloved, building up yourselves on your most holy faith, praying in the Holy Ghost, keep yourselves in the love of God, looking for the mercy of our Lord Jesus Christ unto eternal life. And of some have compassion, making a difference: And others save with fear, pulling them out of the fire; hating even the garment spotted by the flesh. Now unto him that is able to keep you from falling, and to present you faultless before the presence of his glory with exceeding joy, To the only wise God our Saviour, be glory and majesty, dominion and power, both now and ever. Amen." Jude

Abide, Live, Walk In The Consciousness Of The Presence Of God And His Angels

"Let brotherly love continue. Be not forgetful to entertain strangers: for thereby some have entertained angels unawares." Hebrews 13:1-2

Colossians 1:15, 16 "Who (Jesus) is the image of the invisible God, the firstborn of every creature: For by him were all things created, that are in heaven, and that are in earth, visible and invisible, whether they be thrones, or dominions, or principalities, or powers: all things were created by him, and for him: And he is before all things, and by him all things consist."

Revelation 5:6-14 - "And I beheld, and, lo, in the midst of the throne and of the four beasts, and in the midst of the elders, stood a Lamb as it had been slain, having seven horns and seven eyes, which are the seven Spirits of God, sent forth into all the earth. And he came and took the book out of the right hand of him that sat upon the throne. And when he had taken the book, the four beasts and four and twenty elders fell down before the Lamb, having every one of them harps, and golden vials full of odors, which are the prayers of saints.

"And they sung a new song, saying, thou art worthy to take the book, and to open the seals thereof: for thou wast slain, and hast redeemed us to God by thy blood out of every kindred, and tongue, and people, and nation; And hast made us unto our God kings and priests: and we shall reign on the earth.

"And I beheld, and I heard the voice of many angels round about the throne and the beasts and the elders: and the number of them was ten thousand times ten thousand, and thousands of thousands; Saying with a loud voice, Worthy is the Lamb that was slain to receive power, and riches, and wisdom, and strength, and honor, and glory, and blessing.

"And every creature which is in heaven, and on the earth, and under the earth, and such as are in the sea, and all that are in them, heard I saying: Blessing, and honor, and glory, and power, be unto him that sitteth upon the throne, and unto the Lamb forever and ever. And the four beasts said, Amen. And the four and twenty elders fell down and worshipped him that liveth forever and ever."

Do Not Worship Or Bow To Angels

"Blessed are they which are called unto the marriage supper of the Lamb. And he saith unto me, these are the true sayings of God. And I fell at his feet to worship him. And he said unto me, See thou do it not: I am thy fellow servant, and of thy brethren that have the testimony of Jesus: worship God: for the testimony of Jesus is the spirit of prophecy." Revelation 19:7-10

"And I John saw these things and heard them. And when I had heard and seen, I fell down to worship before the feet of the angel which shewed me these things: Then saith he unto me, See thou do it not: for I am thy fellow-servant, and of thy brethren the prophets, and of them which keep the sayings of this book: worship God." Revelation 22:7-9

"I marvel that ye are so soon removed from him that called you into the grace of Christ unto another gospel: Which is not another; but there be some that trouble you and would pervert the gospel of Christ. But though we, or an angel from heaven, preach any other gospel unto you than that which we have preached unto you, let him be accursed." Galatians 1:6-8

"For such are false apostles, deceitful workers, transforming themselves into the apostles of Christ; and no marvel; for Satan himself is transformed into an angel of light. Therefore, it is no great thing if his ministers also be transformed as the ministers of righteousness; whose end shall be according to their works." II Corinthians 11:14, 15

STUDY LESSON VII
WHAT WE BELIEVE

1. **What is Doctrine?** _____

2. **What is the importance on Sound Doctrine?** _____

THE CHRISTIAN FOUNDATION

Name Twelve Bible Doctrines And Define Them Briefly (Use Separate Sheets If Needed)

Biblical Foundation For Spiritual Growth & Maturity

What is the spiritual and physical significance of Biblical Doctrines and the 21st Century?

The Seven Dispensations Seasons Of God's Dealings With Man

Hebrews 1:1 *"God, who at sundry times and in divers manners spoke in time past unto the fathers by the prophets, Hath in these last days spoken unto us by his Son, whom he hath appointed heir of all things, by whom also he made the worlds; Who being the brightness of his glory, and the express image of his person, and upholding all things by the word of his power, when he had by himself purged our sins, sat down on the right hand of the Majesty on high; Being made so much better than the angels, as he hath by inheritance obtained a more excellent name than they."*

Chapter 9
The Seven Dispensations
Seasons Of God's Dealings With Man

Hebrews 1:1-8 - *"God, who at sundry times and in divers manners spoke in time past unto the fathers by the prophets, Hath in these last days spoken unto us by his Son, whom he hath appointed heir of all things, by whom also he made the worlds; Who being the brightness of his glory, and the express image of his person, and upholding all things by the word of his power, when he had by himself purged our sins, sat down on the right hand of the Majesty on high; Being made so much better than the angels, as he hath by inheritance obtained a more excellent name than they."*

Defining Dispensation - Dispensation is defined as:

1. **Different Periods**: Seasons and Times of God's specific dealings with Man

2. **The Ordering of Things:** Specifically: A system of revealed commands, promises regulating human affairs

3. **A Particular Arrangement Or Provision** especially of God's providence or nature

4. **Different Periods Of Time When God Revealed Himself To Man** in different places through difference channels and in different ways. *"God, who at sundry times and in divers manners spake in time past unto the fathers by the prophets, Hath in these last days spoken unto us by [his] Son, whom he hath appointed heir of all things, by whom also he made the worlds;*

"Who being the brightness of His glory, and the express image of his person, and upholding all things by the word of his power, when he had by himself purged our sins, sat down on the right hand of the Majesty on high" Heb 1:1, 2

- **Sundry Times** - Different Times
- **Divers Manners** - Various Ways God Communicated with Man

The Seven Dispensations Of Man
1. Dispensation Of Innocence
2. Dispensation Of Conscience
3. Dispensation Of Human Government (Man In Authority Over The Earth)
4. Dispensation of Promise
5. Dispensation of Law (Theocratic Government of God)
6. Dispensation of Grace
7. The Millennium

1. The First Dispensation - Dispensation Of Innocence
- **Main Characters**: Adam and Eve
- **Scripture:** Genesis 1-3

This dispensation refers to the time when Adam and Eve had no knowledge of the difference between right and wrong and were made caretakers of the Garden of Eden. They sinned against God. They were cursed and driven out of the Garden.

Genesis 3:22-24 Amplified Bible - *"And the Lord God said, "Behold, the man has become like one of Us (Father, Son, Holy Spirit), knowing [how to distinguish between] good and evil; and now, he might stretch out his hand, and take from the tree of life as well, and eat [its fruit], and live [in this fallen, sinful condition] forever" therefore* the Lord God sent Adam away from the Garden of Eden, to till and cultivate the ground from which he was taken. So God drove the man out; and at the east of the Garden of Eden He permanently stationed the Cherubim and the Sword with the flashing blade which turned round and round in every direction to protect and guard the way (entrance, access) to the tree of life."

3. **The Second Dispensation**
   The Dispensation Of Conscience
   - **Main Character:** Noah
   - **Scripture**: Genesis 3-10

This is Noah's Generation. During this dispensation Noah preached for one-hundred and twenty years and only eight souls were saved.
The Period of the knowledge of Good and Evil. The spirit of man died (Separated from God) after the fall.

Genesis 6:1-8 Amplified Bible - *"Now it happened, when men began to multiply on the face of the land, and daughters were born to them, that the sons of God saw that the daughters of men were beautiful and desirable; and they took wives for themselves, whomever they chose and desired. Then the Lord said, "My Spirit shall not strive and remain with man forever, because he is indeed flesh [sinful, corrupt, given over to sensual appetites]; nevertheless, his days shall yet be a hundred and twenty years."*

"There were Nephilim (men of stature, notorious men) on the earth in those days, and also, afterward when the sons of God lived with the daughters of men, and they gave birth

to their children. These were the mighty men who were of old, men of renown (great reputation, fame).
"The Lord saw that the wickedness, depravity of man was great on the earth, and that every imagination or intent of the thoughts of his heart were only evil continually.

"The Lord regretted that He had made mankind on the earth, and He was deeply grieved in His heart. So the Lord said, "I will destroy annihilate) mankind whom I have created from the surface of the earth—not only man, but the animals and the crawling things and the birds of the air because it deeply grieves Me to see mankind's sin and I regret that I have made them. But Noah found favor and grace in the eyes of the Lord."

The Second Dispensation Became The Period When:
1. Satan gained entrance into the soul of man, corrupted him and made him to worship him, the fallen angels, practiced idolatry, witchcraft, sorcery etc.
2. "The Sons of God (fallen angels) got immorally involved with the daughters of men
3. Man lived by the dictates of his conscience
4. God judged this generation by restraining the Holy Spirit from striving with man and by a great flood

3. The Third Dispensation - The Dispensation Of Human Government (Man In Authority Over The Earth)
- **Main Character:** Nimrod
- **The Period Of Time After The Great Flood**
- **References**: Genesis 10-11

The main character for this dispensation was Nimrod. This was the period of continual worship of Satan, and the fallen angels. It also gave birth to human worship. Nimrod (the name meaning, we will rebel) mobilized his generation to live in colonization and built the first cities of the earth. The beginning of his kingdom was Babel (the gate of gods), Erech, Accad, Calneh in the Land of Shinar. Babel, later became Babylon. The Tower of Babel was an open defiance and rebellion against the God of creation. God ended this dispensation when he visited the tower and confused their tongue by giving them multiple languages and scattered them over the face of the earth.

After the death of Nimrod, Samaramis, Nimrod's wife, claimed to be pregnant by the god's. She gave birth to a son and named him,Tamuz and introduced him as Nimrod reincarnated. She deified Tamuz. Images were then erected to represent Nimrod, Samaramis amd Tamuz. The images of Father, Son and Mother we see in some Churches and religious places originated from this period of human worship.

Nimrod was the founder of the first City, Babel. Babel means the gate of gods. This was a portal to the realms of the spirit. It was surrounded by idols, images designed to fight against God. It was at this time when God came down and confused the tongues of men. This confusion resulted in the diversity of languages.

Genesis 10:8-10 - "And Cush begat Nimrod: he began to be a mighty one in the earth. He was a mighty hunter before the LORD: wherefore it is said, Even as Nimrod the mighty hunter before the LORD. And the beginning of his kingdom was Babel, and Erech, and Accad, and Calneh, in the land of Shinar."

Genesis 11:1-9 - *"And the whole earth was of one language, and of one speech. And it came to pass, as they journeyed from the east, that they found a plain in the land of Shinar; and they dwelt there. And they said one to another, Go to, let us make brick, and burn them thoroughly. And they had brick for stone, and slime had they for mortar. And they said, Go to, let us build us a city and a tower, whose top [may reach] unto heaven; and let us make us a name, lest we be scattered abroad upon the face of the whole earth.*

"And the LORD came down to see the city and the tower, which the children of men builded. And the LORD said, Behold, the people [is] one, and they have all one language; and this they begin to do: and now nothing will be restrained from them, which they have imagined to do. Go to, let us go down, and there confound their language, that they may not understand one another's speech. So the LORD scattered them abroad from thence upon the face of all the earth: and they left off to build the city. Therefore is the name of it called Babel; because the LORD did there confound the language of all the earth: and from thence did the LORD scatter them abroad upon the face of all the earth."

4. The Fourth Dispensation – Dispensation Of Promise Or Man Under Promise
- **Main Character:** Abram (Abraham)
- **Scriptures:** Genesis 12 - Exodus 18
- God Raised A Nation Out Of Abraham's Seed - Isaac.

This is the Period God called Abraham out of Ur of the Chaldees and established (Cut) a blood covenant with him. God blessed Abraham and promised to raise a new Nation (a new generation) of people, who will worship him as the only One true God.

God promised to give his descendants a land, Bless them and make them a Blessing to Nations. Abraham gave birth to Isaac. Isaac gave birth to Jacob. Jacob and his twelve sons - the twelve Patriarchs, settled in Egypt after Joseph had been made the Prime Minister. The Nation of Israel was birthed in Egypt. For seventy years they lived in slavery, in anticipation of a deliverer who would rise to fulfill God's promise given to Abraham, to lead them out of slavery and bondage into their own land (the promised land) - Canaan. God raised Moses and with a strong and mighty hand delivered them from Pharaoh. In the wilderness, on Mt. Sinai, Moses received the ten commandments: marking the end of the dispensation of Promise (the fourth dispensation), and then, beginning the fifth dispensation (the dispensation of Law). Not any Law but God's Law. According to Galatians chapter three, verse seven through nine: Gentiles who are not direct descendants of Abraham were blessed in Abraham at the time of this covenant.

Galatians 3:6-9 - "Even as Abraham believed God, and it was accounted to him for righteousness. Know ye therefore that they which are of faith, the same are the children of Abraham. And the scripture foreseeing that God would justify [declare righteous, put in write standing with Himself] the heathen through faith, preached before Gentiles in consequence of faith, proclaiming the gospel [foretelling the glad tidings of a Savior ling beforehand] to Abraham in the promise, saying: In you shall all the nations of the earth be blessed.

Galatians 3:13-29 - "Christ hath redeemed us from the curse of the law, being made a curse for us: for it is written, Cursed is every one that hangeth on a tree: That the blessing of Abraham might come on the Gentiles through Jesus Christ; that we might receive the promise of the Spirit through faith...For ye are all the children of God by faith in Christ Jesus. For as many of you as have been baptized into Christ have put on Christ. There is neither Jew nor Greek, there is neither bond nor free, there is neither male nor female: for ye are all one in Christ Jesus. And if ye be Christ's, then are ye Abraham's seed, and heirs according to the promise." Though the LORD God blessed Abraham years ago, everyone who is not a direct descendant of Abraham (Gentile), who believes in Jesus and accept Him as personal Lord and Savior becomes a child of faith and hence the seed of Abraham.

5. The Fifth Dispensation: The Dispensation Of Law
- **Main Character**: Moses
- **Scriptures:** Exodus 19 - Malachi 4:6

This was not the law of men, but the Law of the Theocratic Government of Jehovah given on Mt. Sinai. God gave unto Moses, the Ten Commandments, Statutes and Ordinances.

The success, progress and establishment of this new nation over their enemies and possession of their land depended on their obedience to the One True God. Every allegiance to the governments and gods of Egypt and the nations they will conquer was to be broken and utterly destroyed. No diplomatic relationship with the gods of the land. Israel inherited the land of Canaan. Unfortunately, among those who left Egypt, only two could reach Canaan, the rest were destroyed because they were deceived by their own lust, mummering, complaining, un-faithlessness, disobedience, rebellion, etc. The period extended through the time of the Judges, Kings, and Priests until the time of Jesus Crucifixion and resurrection.

6. The Sixth Dispensation
The Dispensation Of Grace (Unmerited Favor)
- Main Character: Jesus Christ
- Scripture: The New Testament

We are presently living in the dispensation of Grace. Grace means: unmerited favor (God's Unmerited Favor). Favor, we did not deserve - the death, burial and resurrection of Jesus Christ gave man, redemption, freedom. The power of sin, iniquity, curse and death - separation from God, has been broken, and has no more control over man because of the death and resurrection of Jesus Christ.

"And you were dead in your trespasses and sins, in which you formerly walked according to the course of this world, according to the prince of the power of the air, of the spirit that is now working in the sons of disobedience. Among them we too all formerly lived in the lusts of our flesh, indulging the desires of the flesh and of the mind, and were by nature children of wrath, even as the rest. But God, being rich in mercy, because of His great love with which He loved us, even when we were dead in our transgressions, made us alive together with Christ (by grace you have been saved), and raised us up with Him, and seated us with Him in the heavenly places in Christ

Jesus, so that in the ages to come He might show the surpassing riches of His grace in kindness toward us in Christ Jesus. For by grace you have been saved through faith; and that not of yourselves, it is the gift of God; not as a result of works, so that no one may boast. For we are His workmanship, created in Christ Jesus for good works, which God prepared beforehand so that we would walk in them." Ephesians 2:1-10

7. The Millennial Reign Of Christ Jesus On Earth
- **Main Character:** Jesus Christ During His 1000-Year Reign On Earth
- **Scripture:** Revelation 20

This is the thousand-year reign of Christ Jesus on Earth. During this time Satan will be band for one thousand years. This period will be the last period of God's Government on earth, before the Consummation - the final judgment of the earth. It will be after the battle of Armageddon.

"And I saw an angel come down from heaven, having the key of the bottomless pit and a great chain in his hand. And he laid hold on the dragon, that old serpent, which is the Devil, and Satan, and bound him a thousand years, And cast him into the bottomless pit, and shut him up, and set a seal upon him, that he should deceive the nations no more, till the thousand years should be fulfilled: and after that he must be loosed a little season. And I saw thrones, and they sat upon them, and judgment was given unto them: and I saw the souls of them that were beheaded for the witness of Jesus, and for the word of God, and which had not worshipped the beast, neither his image, neither had received his mark upon their foreheads, or in their hands;

and they lived and reigned with Christ a thousand years. But the rest of the dead lived not again until the thousand years were finished. This is the first resurrection. Blessed and holy is he that hath part in the first resurrection: on such the second death hath no power, but they shall be priests of God and of Christ and shall reign with him a thousand years. And when the thousand years are expired, Satan shall be loosed out of his prison and shall go out to deceive the nations which are in the four quarters of the earth, Gog and Magog, to gather them together to battle: the number of whom is as the sand of the sea. And they went up on the breadth of the earth, and compassed the camp of the saints about, and the beloved city: and fire came down from God out of heaven and devoured them. And the devil that deceived them was cast into the lake of fire and brimstone, where the beast and the false prophet are, and shall be tormented day and night forever and ever. And I saw a great white throne, and him that sat on it, from whose face the earth and the heaven fled away; and there was found no place for them.

"And I saw the dead, small and great, stand before God; and the books were opened: and another book was opened, which is the book of life: and the dead were judged out of those things which were written in the books, according to their works. And the sea gave up the dead which were in it; and death and hell delivered up the dead which were in them: and they were judged every man according to their works. And death and hell were cast into the lake of fire. This is the second death. And whosoever was not found written in the book of life was cast into the lake of fire."
Revelation 20

THE CHRISTIAN FOUNDATION

Study Lesson VIII
The Seven Dispensations

1. What is dispensation? _____

2. How many dispensations are there? _____

4. In which dispensation are we living in Now? _____

5. What is the name of the dispensation in which we live?
_____

5. How many sons did Jacob have? _____

6. Who was Jacob's favorite wife? _____

7. Who were Jacob's favorite sons? _____

and _____ Why? _____

8. Name all of the dispensations and their main characters
  1) _____ _____
  2) _____ _____
  3) _____ _____
  4) _____ _____
  5) _____ _____
  6) _____ _____

7)

Financial Stewardship

Deuteronomy 8:18 "But thou shalt remember the LORD thy God: for it is he that giveth thee power to get wealth, that he may establish his covenant which he swore unto thy fathers, as it is this day."

Isaiah 45:2-3 "I will go before thee and make the crooked places straight: I will break in pieces the gates of brass and cut in sunder the bars of iron: And I will give thee the treasures of darkness, and hidden riches of secret places, that thou mayest know that I, the LORD, which call thee by thy name, am the God of Israel."

Chapter 10
Financial Stewardship Principles

Genesis 1:27-31 (Amplified Bible) *"So God created man in His own image, in the image and likeness of God He created him; male and female He created them. And God blessed them [granting them certain authority] and said to them, "Be fruitful, multiply, and fill the earth, and subjugate it [putting it under your power]; and rule over (dominate) the fish of the sea, the birds of the air, and every living thing that moves upon the earth."*

"So God said: Behold, I have given you every plant yielding seed that is on the surface of the entire earth, and every tree which has fruit yielding seed; it shall be food for you; and to all the animals on the earth and to every bird of the air and to everything that moves on the ground, to everything in which there is the breath of life, I have given every green plant for food"; and it was so [because He commanded it]. God saw everything that He had made, and behold, it was very good, and He validated it completely."

Dominion Defined - Dominion is ownership, rulership, kingdom or governmental rule. Dominion is power and authority. When you are in full control or in full charge of anything, you rule it, you have dominion.

The Biblical context of Dominion transcends, goes beyond the limits of the natural and the supernatural. When man submits to the Counsel of God, he has Dominion: He rules both the natural and the supernatural.

THE CHRISTIAN FOUNDATION

This is a Serious Order of Blessing. God's Original Thought and Counsel for "Man" - *"And God blessed them [granting them certain authority] and said to them, "Be fruitful, multiply, and fill the earth, and subjugate it [putting it under your power]; and rule over (dominate) the fish of the sea, the birds of the air, and every living thing that moves upon the earth."*

Prosperity Defined - Prosperity is generally defined as the condition of being successful or thriving, *especially* in the context of economic well-being. But Biblical Prosperity is more than that. The Human Being is a Tripartite Being (Spirit, Soul and Body), Originally Created by the Most-High God to be the sole administrator and caretaker of God's Creation. God created Man to have dominion over all creation, celestial, terrestrial, and the underworld. Definitely, Economic, freedom and emancipation is indeed part of God's bigger picture of Dominion and Prosperity. True Dominion and Economic Prosperity always walks with God's Wisdom, so in the end God's Character and agenda is manifested. Solomon said:

Ecclesiastes 10:19c "...Money Answers All Things." And Ecclesiastes 11:12 "Wisdom is good with an inheritance: and by it there is profit to them that see the sun. For wisdom is a defense, and Money Is A Defense: but the excellency of knowledge is, that wisdom giveth life to them that have it"

Ecclesiastes 10:5-7 "There is an evil which I have seen under the sun, as an error which proceedeth from the ruler: Folly is set in great dignity, and the rich sit in low place. I have seen servants upon horses, and princes walking as servants upon the earth."

Dominion Mandate & Economic Prosperity Is Repeated In Genesis 8:1, 20-22; 9:1-7

Genesis 8:1, 20-22 & 9:1-7 - *"And God remembered Noah, and every living thing, and all the cattle that was with him in the ark: and God made a wind to pass over the earth, and the waters asswaged... And Noah built an altar unto the LORD; and took of every clean beast, and of every clean fowl, and offered burnt offerings on the altar. And the LORD smelled a sweet savor; and the LORD said in his heart, I will not again curse the ground any more for man's sake; for the imagination of man's heart is evil from his youth; neither will I again smite any more everything living, as I have done. While the earth remained, seedtime and harvest, and cold and heat, and summer and winter, and day and night shall not cease."*

Genesis 9:1-7 *"And God blessed Noah and his sons, and said unto them: Be fruitful, and multiply, and replenish the earth. And the fear of you and the dread of you shall be upon every beast of the earth, and upon every fowl of the air, upon all that moves upon the earth, and upon all the fishes of the sea; into your hand are they delivered. Every moving thing that lives shall be meat for you; even as the green herb have I given you all things... And you, be ye fruitful, and multiply; bring forth abundantly in the earth, and multiply therein."*

It's God's Will To Succeed And Prosper - ***Deuteronomy 8:18*** **-** *"But thou shalt remember the LORD thy God: for it is he that giveth thee power to get wealth, that he may establish his covenant which he swore unto thy fathers, as it is this day."*

Deuteronomy 28:1-14 *"And it shall come to pass, if thou shalt hearken diligently unto the voice of the LORD thy God, to observe and to do all his commandments which I command thee this day, that the LORD thy God will set thee on high above all nations of the earth: And all these blessings shall come on thee, and overtake thee, if thou shalt hearken unto the voice of the LORD thy God.*

"Blessed shalt thou be in the city, and blessed shalt thou be in the field. Blessed shall be the fruit of thy body, and the fruit of thy ground, and the fruit of thy cattle, the increase of thy kine, and the flocks of thy sheep. Blessed shall be thy basket and thy store. Blessed shalt thou be when thou comest in, and blessed shalt thou be when thou goest out. The LORD shall cause thine enemies that rise up against thee to be smitten before thy face: they shall come out against thee one way, and flee before thee seven ways. The LORD shall command the blessing upon thee in thy storehouses, and in all that thou settest thine hand unto; and he shall bless thee in the land which the LORD thy God giveth thee.

"The LORD shall establish thee an holy people unto himself, as he hath sworn unto thee, if thou shalt keep the commandments of the LORD thy God, and walk in his ways. And all people of the earth shall see that thou art called by the name of the LORD; and they shall be afraid of thee. And the LORD shall make thee plenteous in goods, in the fruit of thy body, and in the fruit of thy cattle, and in the fruit of thy ground, in the land which the LORD swore unto thy fathers to give thee. The LORD shall open unto thee his good treasure, the heaven to give the rain unto thy land in his season, and to bless all the work of thine hand:

and thou shalt lend unto many nations, and thou shalt not borrow. And the LORD shall make thee the head, and not the tail; and thou shalt be above only, and thou shalt not be beneath; if that thou hearken unto the commandments of the LORD thy God, which I command thee this day, to observe and to do them: And thou shalt not go aside from any of the words which I command thee this day, to the right hand, or to the left, to go after other gods to serve them."

Ecclesiastes 9:11 *- "I again saw under the sun that the race is not to the swift and the battle is not to the strong, and neither is bread to the wise nor riches to those of intelligence and understanding nor favor to men of ability; but time and chance overtake them all."*

Ecclesiastes 10:5-7 *"There is an evil which I have seen under the sun, as an error which proceeds from the ruler: Folly is set in great dignity, and the rich sit in low place. I have seen servants upon horses, and princes walking as servants upon the earth."*

III John 1:2 *- "Beloved, I pray that in every way you may succeed and prosper and be in good health physically, just as I know your soul prospers spiritually.*

God Jehovah Is Sovereign - Psalm 24:1-2 - *"The earth is the LORD's, and the fulness thereof; the world, and they that dwell therein. For he hath founded it upon the seas and established it upon the floods."*

1Thessolonians 5:23 - *"And the very God of peace sanctify you wholly; and I pray God your whole spirit and* *soul and body be preserved blameless unto the coming of our Lord Jesus Christ. Faithful is he that calleth you, who also will do it."*

All Of God's Creation & The Planet Earth Are Subject to Man, Not Angels – Hebrews 2:5-14 (From Psalm 8) (The Amplified Bible)

"It was not to angels that God subjected the [inhabited] world of the future [when Christ reigns], about which we are speaking. But one has [solemnly] testified somewhere [in Scripture], saying

"What is man, that You are mindful of him, Or the son of man, that You graciously care for him? You have made him for a little while lower [in status] than the angels; You have crowned him with glory and honor and set him over the works of Your hands.

"You have put all things in subjection under his feet [confirming his supremacy]. Now in putting all things in subjection to man, He left nothing outside his control. But at present we do not yet see all things subjected to him.

"But we do see Jesus, who was made lower than the angels for a little while [by taking on the limitations of humanity], crowned with glory and honor because of His suffering of death, so that by the grace of God [extended to sinners] He might experience death for [the sins of] everyone.

"For it was fitting for God [that is, an act worthy of His divine nature] that He, for whose sake are all things, and through whom are all things, in bringing many sons to

glory, should make the author and founder of their salvation perfect through suffering [bringing to maturity the human experience necessary for Him to be perfectly equipped for His office as High Priest].

It Is God's Will To Prosper You

1. *"But thou shalt remember the LORD thy God: for it is he that giveth thee power to get wealth, that he may establish his covenant which he swore unto thy fathers, as it is this day" - Deuteronomy 8:18*

2. *III John 1:2 - "Beloved, I wish above all things that thou mayest prosper and be in health, even as thy soul prospereth"*

3. *Haggai 2:8 - "The silver is mine, and the gold is mine, saith the LORD of hosts"*

4. *Psalm 50:10 - "For every beast of the forest is mine, and the cattle upon a thousand hills"*

5. *Matthew 6:25-32 - "Therefore I say unto you: Take no thought for your life, what ye shall eat, or what ye shall drink; nor yet for your body, what ye shall put on. Is not the life more than meat, and the body than raiment?*

   "Behold the fowls of the air: for they sow not, neither do they reap, nor gather into barns; yet your heavenly Father feedeth them. Are ye not much better than they? Which of you by taking thought can add one cubit unto his stature? And why take ye thought for raiment?

"Consider the lilies of the field, how they grow; they toil not, neither do they spin: And yet I say unto you, that even Solomon in all his glory was not arrayed like one of these.

"Wherefore, if God so clothe the grass of the field, which today is, and tomorrow is cast into the oven, shall he not much more clothe you, O ye of little faith? Therefore, take no thought, saying, what shall we eat? Or what shall we drink? Or wherewithal shall we be clothed? For after all these things do the Gentiles seek: for your heavenly Father knoweth that ye have need of all these things"

6. II Corinthians 8:9 – "For ye know the grace of our Lord Jesus Christ, that, though he was rich, yet for your sakes he became poor, that ye through his poverty might be rich."

7. II Corinthians 9:8-11 – "And God is able to make all grace abound toward you; that ye, always having all sufficiency in all things, may abound to every good work: (As it is written, He hath dispersed abroad; he hath given to the poor: his righteousness remaineth forever.

"Now he that ministereth seed to the sower both minister bread for your food, and multiply your seed sown, and increase the fruits of your righteousness;)

"Being enriched in everything to all bountifulness, which causeth through us thanksgiving to God."

Biblical Steps Into Financial Emancipation

I. **Acknowledge That God Is The Source Of Life For All Creation And The Ultimate Supplier Of All Things**

a. *Deuteronomy 8:18* "*But thou shalt remember the LORD thy God: for it is he that giveth thee power to get wealth, that he may establish his covenant which he sware unto thy fathers, as it is this day.*"

b. *Philippians 4:19* "*But my God shall supply all your needs according to his riches in glory by Christ Jesus*"

c. *II Corinthians 9:8* "*And God is able to make all grace abound toward you; that ye, always having all sufficiency in all things, may abound to every good work*"

d. *Matthew 14:20* "*And they did all eat, and were filled: and they took up of the fragments that remained twelve baskets full*"

e. *Ephesians 3:20* "*Now unto him that is able to do exceedingly abundantly above all that we ask or think according to the power that worketh in us*"

f. *Psalm 127:1-2* "*Except the LORD build the house, they labor in vain that build it: except the LORD keep the city, the watchman waketh but in vain. It is vain for you to rise up early, to sit up late, to eat the bread of sorrows: for so he giveth his beloved sleep*"

II. Believe That God Has Already Made The Provision For Your Success

a. **II Peter1:3** *"According as his divine power hath given unto us all things that pertain unto life and godliness, through the knowledge of him that hath called us to glory and virtue"*

b. **Proverbs 13:22** *"A good man leaveth an inheritance to his children's children: and the wealth of the sinner is laid up for the just"*

III. Biblical Principles On Giving

Tithes & Offerings

Tithes and offerings are fundamental aspects of Christian stewardship, demonstrating our love, gratitude, and obedience to God.

Tithes Defined - Tithe is the tenth of one's income, set apart as a sacred portion for God (Leviticus 27:30-32; Numbers 18:21-24).

Malachi 3:10 "*Bring ye all the tithes into the storehouse, that there may be meat in mine house, and prove me now herewith, saith the LORD of hosts, if I will not open you the windows of heaven, and pour you out a blessing, that there shall not be room enough to receive it. And I will rebuke the devourer for your sakes, and he shall not destroy the fruits of your ground; neither shall your vine cast her fruit before the time in the field, saith the LORD of hosts.*

"And all nations shall call you blessed: for ye shall be a delightsome land, saith the LORD of hosts."

Purpose: To support the Church, Ministry, Ministers, and the Poor, demonstrating our gratitude for God's Provision and Blessings (Deuteronomy 14:22-29; 26:12-15)

Biblical Examples:
1. Abraham- Genesis 14:20
2. Jacob Genesis 28:20-22
3. Israelites - Leviticus 27:30-32 - all practiced tithing

New Testament Perspective: While the New Testament doesn't explicitly command tithing, it emphasizes the importance of generous giving, cheerfulness, and putting God first - Matthew 23:23; 2 Corinthians 9:6-7

1. Be Obedience In Tithing & Offering

a. **Tithe Is On The Gross Income** - Proverbs 3:9-10 *"Honor the LORD with thy substance, and with the first fruits of all thine increase: So shall thy barns be filled with plenty, and thy presses shall burst out with new wine"* Exodus 23:19a *"The first of the first fruits of thy land thou shalt bring into the house of the LORD thy God"*

b. **Tithes Belong To God** - Leviticus 27:30 *"And all the tithe of the land, whether of the seed of the land, or of the fruit of the tree, is the LORD'S: it is holy unto the LORD"*

THE CHRISTIAN FOUNDATION

c. **To Refuse To Tithe Is To Rob God** - *"Will a man rob God? Yet ye have robbed me. But ye say, wherein have we robbed thee? In tithes and offerings:" - Malachi 3:8.*

d. **Tithe Should Go To Where You Are Spiritually Fed And Catered For** - *Malachi 3:10 "Bring ye all the tithes into the storehouse, that there may be meat in mine house, and prove me now herewith, saith the LORD of hosts, if I will not open you the windows of heaven, and pour you out a blessing, that there shall not be room enough to receive it"*

e. **Jesus Taught Tithing Is Both Old And New Testament.** - **Matthew 23:23** *"Woe unto you, scribes and Pharisees, hypocrites! for ye pay tithe of mint and anise and cummin, and have omitted the weightier matters of the law, judgment, mercy, and faith: these ought ye to have done, and not to leave the other undone"*

f. **God Is Our First Debtor (Pay Tithe First)** - **Matthew 6:33** *"But seek ye first the kingdom of God, and his righteousness; and all these things shall be added unto you"* -

g. **God Challenges Us To Put Him To The Test** - Malachi 3:10 *"Bring ye all the tithes into the storehouse, that there may be meat in mine house, and prove me now herewith, saith the LORD of hosts, if I will not open you the windows of heaven, and pour you out a blessing, that there shall not be room enough to receive it"*

h. **God Promises To Rebuke The Devourer For Us**
   Malachi 3:11 *"And I will rebuke the devourer for your sakes, and he shall not destroy the fruits of your ground; neither shall your vine cast her fruit before the time in the field, saith the LORD of hosts"*

2. Do Not Give In Fear - Free-Will Offering - Personal Decision Made In The Fear And Respect Of God

a. **Exodus 35:5,21** *"Take ye from among you an offering unto the LORD: whosoever is of a willing heart, let him bring it, an offering of the LORD; gold, and silver and brass... They came, everyone whose heart stirred him up, and everyone whom his spirit makes willing, and they brought the LORD's offering to the work of the tabernacle of the congregation, and for all his service"*

b. **Exodus 36:5,7** *"And they spoke unto Moses, saying, the people bring much more than enough for the* service of the *work, which the LORD commanded to make... "For the stuff they had was sufficient for all the work to make it, and too much"*

c. **Acts 20:35** *"I have showed you all things, how that so laboring ye ought to support the week, and to remember the words of the Lord Jesus, how he said, it is more blessed to give than to receive"*

3. Give Generously & In Faith

Ecclesiastes 11:1-6 *"Cast thy bread upon the waters: for thou shalt find it after many days... He that observeth the wind shall not sow; and he that regardeth the clouds shall* *not reap. As thou knowest not what is the way of the spirit, nor how the bones do grow in the womb of her that is with child: even so thou knowest not the works of God who maketh all. In the morning sow thy seed, and in the evening withhold not thine hand: for thou knowest not whether shall prosper, either this or that, or whether they both shall be alike good."*

Luke 6:38 "*Give, and it shall be given unto you; good measure, pressed down, and shaken together, and running over, shall men give into your bosom. For with the same measure that ye mete withal it shall be measured to you again*"

4. Don't Give Just Because There Is A Need Or Necessity Give Cheerfully. Give In Faith Believing That God Will Produce The Harvest

II Corinthians 9:6-14 "But this I say, He which soweth sparingly shall reap also sparingly; and he which soweth bountifully shall reap also bountifully. *Every man according as he purposeth in his heart, so let him give; not grudgingly, or of necessity: for God loveth a cheerful giver. And God is able to make all grace abound toward you; that ye, always having all sufficiency in all things, may abound to every good work:(As it is written, He hath dispersed abroad; he hath given to the poor: his righteousness remaineth forever. He that ministereth seed to the sower both minister bread for your food, and multiply your seed sown, and increase the fruits of your righteousness;) enriched in everything to all bountifulness, which causeth through us thanksgiving to God. For the administration of this service not only supplieth the want of the saints but is* *abundant also by many thanksgivings unto God. Whiles by the experiment of this ministration they glorify God for your professed subjection unto the gospel of Christ, and for your liberal distribution unto them, and unto all men; And by their prayer for you, which long after you for the exceeding grace of God in you"*

5. Give With Good & Honorable Motive

Exodus 25:1 *"And the LORD spake unto Moses, saying: Speak unto the children of Israel, that they bring me an offering: of every man that giveth it willingly with his heart ye shall take my offering."*

6. Give Generously - *Proverbs 11:24-25* "There is that scattereth, and yet increaseth; and there is that withhold more than is meet, but it tendeth to poverty. The liberal soul shall be made fat: and he that watereth shall be watered also himself"

7. Be A Good Steward In All Things. Worship God Freely With Whatever You Have. In the parable of the talents, we find the principle of use it or lose it

a. **Exodus 4:2** *"And the LORD said unto him, what is that in thine hand? And he said, A rod"*

b. **I Kings 17:10-16** *"Elijah asked the widow to use her last meal and oil to fix him a cake.*

c. **Mark 6:38-41** *"He saith unto them, how many loaves have ye? Go and see. And when they knew, they say, five, and two fishes. He commanded them to make all* *sit down by companies upon the green grass. And they sat down in ranks, by hundreds, and by fifties. And when he had taken the five loaves and the two fishes, he looked up to heaven, and blessed, and broke the loaves, and gave them to his disciples to set before them; and the two fishes divided he among them all"*

8. Don't Buy or Act On Impulse - Do Not Allow Fear To Manipulate And Control Your Financial Decisions. As Much As Possible Do Not Borrow

a. Romans 13:8 *"Owe no man anything, but to love one another: for he that loveth another hath fulfilled the law"*

b. Proverbs 22:7 *"The rich runleth over the poor and the borrower is servant to the lender"*

To "owe" brings one under mental bondage. From the moment we sign till be pay, the burden rests in our minds. *Matthew 6:34 "Take therefore no thought for the morrow: for the morrow shall take thought for the things of itself. Sufficient unto the day is the evil thereof"*

c. Philippians 4:19 *"But my God shall supply all your need according to his riches in glory by Christ Jesus"*

d. Proverbs 17:18 *"A man void of understanding strikes hands, and becometh surety in the presence of his friend"*

e. Haggai 2:8 *"The silver is mine, and the gold is mine, saith the LORD of hosts"*

9. Exercise Self-Control: Avoid Get-Rich-Quick Schemes

a. Proverbs 14:29 "He that is slow to wrath is of great understanding: but he that is hasty of spirit exalteth folly"

b. Prov. 21:25 "The thoughts of the diligent tend only to plenteousness but of everyone that is hasty only to want"

c. Proverbs 27:12 "A prudent man foreseeth the evil, and hideth himself; but the simple pass on, and are punished"

b. Proverbs 28:19, 22 "He that tilleth his land shall have plenty of bread: but he that followeth after vain persons shall have poverty enough"

c. Proverbs 28:19, 22 "He that hasteth to be rich hath an evil eye, and considereth not that poverty shall come upon him"

10. Allow God's Word To Be Your Guide

a. Proverbs 12:15 "The way of a fool is right in his own eyes: but he that hearkeneth unto counsel is wise" Proverbs 13:18 "Poverty and shame shall be to him that refuseth instruction: but he that regardeth reproof shall be honoured"

b. Proverbs 15:22 "Without counsel purposes are disappointed: but in the multitude of counselors, they are established"

11. Check Your Attitude Towards Money

a. **Don't Be Selfish** - *Prov. 11:24-25* "There is that scattereth, and yet increaseth; and there is that withholdeth more than is meet, but it tendeth to poverty. The liberal soul shall be made fat: and he that watereth shall be watered also himself"

b. **Don't Be Dishonest** - *Proverbs 20:23* "Divers weights are an abomination unto the LORD; and a false balance is not good"

Proverbs 28:8 "He that by usury and unjust gain increaseth his substance, he shall gather it for him that will pity the poor"

c. **Don't Be Greedy** - *Proverbs 15:27* "He that is greedy of gain troubleth his own house; but he that hateth gifts shall live"

d. **Don't Love Money Above God** - *I Timothy 6:10* "For the love of money is the root of all evil: which while some coveted after, they have erred from the faith, and pierced themselves through with many sorrows"

Cultivate A Good Attitude Towards Work

Prov. 10:4 "He becometh poor that dealeth with a slack hand: but the hand of the diligent maketh rich"

Proverbs 13:4 "The soul of the sluggard desireth, and hath nothing: but the soul of the diligent shall be made fat"

Proverbs 12:24 "The hand of the diligent shall bear rule: but the slothful shall be under tribute"

Proverbs 18:9 "He also that is slothful in his work is brother to him that is a great waster"

Proverbs 21:25 "The desire of the slothful killeth him; for his hands refuse to labor"

II Thess. 3:10 "For even when we were with you, this we commanded you, that if any would not work, neither should he eat"

Proverbs 23:4 "Labor not to be rich: cease from thine own wisdom"

Proverbs 22:29 "Seest thou a man diligent in his business? He shall stand before kings; he shall not stand before mean men"

Proverbs 23:21 "For the drunkard and the glutton shall come to poverty: and drowsiness shall clothe a man with rags"

To Be Content With What God Has Provided You

Philippians 4:11 "Not that I speak in respect of want for I have learned, in whatsoever state I am, therewith to be content" I Timothy 6:8 "And having food and raiment let us be therewith content"

Give To The Disadvantaged And The Poor

a. *Proverbs 19:17 "He that hath pity upon the poor tendeth unto the LORD; and that which he hath given will he pay him again"*

b. *Proverbs 21:13 "Whoso stoppeth his ears at the cry of the poor, he also shall cry himself, but shall not be heard"*

c. *Proverbs 22:9 "He that hath a bountiful eye shall be blessed; for he giveth of his bread to the poor"*

d. *Proverbs 22:16 "He that oppresseth the poor to increase his riches, and he that giveth to the rich, shall surely come to want"*

e. *Proverbs. 28:27 "He that giveth unto the poor shall not lack but he that hideth his eyes shall have many a curse"*

f. *Matthew 19:21 "Jesus said unto him, if thou wilt be perfect, go and sell that thou hast, and give to the poor, and thou shalt have treasure in heaven: and come and follow me"*

g. Acts 2:41-47 *"Then they that gladly received his word were baptized: and the same day there were added unto them about three thousand souls. And they continued steadfastly in the apostles' doctrine and fellowship, and in breaking of bread, and in prayers. And fear came upon every soul: and many wonders and signs were done by the apostles. And all that believed were together and had all things common; And sold their possessions and goods, and parted them to all men, as every man had need.*

"And they, continuing daily with one accord in the temple, and breaking bread from house to house, did eat their meat with gladness and singleness of heart, Praising God, and having favour with all the people. And the Lord added to the church daily such as should be saved."

h. Acts 4:21-35 *"And when they had prayed, the place was shaken where they were assembled together; and they were all filled with the Holy Ghost, and they spake the word of God with boldness. And the multitude of them that believed were of one heart and of one soul: neither said any of them that ought of the things which he possessed was his own; but they had all things common. And with great power gave the apostles witness of the resurrection of the Lord Jesus: and great grace was upon them all.*
"Neither was there any among them that lacked: for as many as were possessors of lands or houses sold them and brought the prices of the things that were sold and laid them down at the apostles' feet: and distribution was made unto every man according as he had need."

Ask God In Faith For The Release Of Your Financial Breakthrough

"For verily I say unto you, that whosoever shall say unto this mountain: Be thou removed, and be thou cast into the sea; and shall not doubt in his heart, but shall believe that those things which he saith shall come to pass; he shall have whatsoever he saith" Mark 11:23

Hebrews 11:6 *"But without faith it is impossible to please him: for he that cometh to God must believe that he is, and that he is a rewarder of them that diligently seek him."*

The Benefits Of Prayer And Fasting In Financial Freedom And Integrity

Isaiah 58:6-14 - *"Is it not the fast that I have chosen:*
- *To lose the bands of wickedness*
- *To undo the heavy burdens*
- *To let the oppressed, go free*
- *That ye break every yoke?*
- *Is it not to deal thy bread to the hungry?*
- *That thou bring the poor that are cast out to thy house?*
- *When thou seest the naked, that thou cover him*
- *That thou hide not thyself from thine own flesh*
- *Then shall thy light break forth as the morning*
- *Thine health shall spring forth speedily*
- *Thy righteousness shall go before thee*
- *The glory of the LORD shall be thy rereward*
- *Then shalt thou call, and the LORD shall answer.*
- *Thou shalt cry, and he shall say, Here I am.*

- *If thou take away from the midst of thee the yoke, the putting forth of the finger, and speaking vanity*
- *And if thou draw out thy soul to the hungry, and satisfy the afflicted soul*
- *Then shall thy light rise in obscurity*
- *Thy darkness be as the noonday*
- *The LORD shall guide thee continually, and satisfy thy soul in drought, and make fat thy bones*
- *Thou shalt be like a watered garden, and like a spring of water, whose waters fail not.*
- *They that shall be of thee shall build the old waste places*
- *Thou shalt raise up the foundations of many generations*
- *Thou shalt be called, the repairer of the breach*
- *The restorer of paths to dwell i*
- *If thou turn away thy foot from the sabbath, from doing thy pleasure on my holy day; and call the sabbath a delight, the holy of the LORD, honorable; and shalt honour him, not doing thine own ways, nor finding thine own pleasure, nor speaking thine own words: shalt thou delight thyself in the LORD*
- *I will cause thee to ride upon the high places of the earth and Feed thee with the heritage of Jacob thy father: for the mouth of the LORD hath spoken it"*

Malachi 3:3 *"And he shall sit as a refiner and purifier of silver: and he shall purify the sons of Levi, and purge them as gold and silver, that they may offer unto the LORD an offering in righteousness"*

Joshua 1:8 "This book of the law shall not depart out of thy mouth; but thou shalt meditate therein day and night, that thou mayest observe to do according to all that is written therein: for then thou shalt make thy way prosperous, and then thou shalt have good success"

Psalm 92:12 "The righteous shall flourish like the palm tree: he shall grow like a cedar in Lebanon."

Joshua 1:3 "Every place that the sole of your foot shall tread upon, that have I given unto you, as I said unto Moses"

Psalm 37:4 "Delight thyself also in the LORD; and he shall give thee the desires of thine heart."

Psalms 37:25 "I have been young, and now am old; yet have I not seen the righteous forsaken, nor his seed begging bread."

Matthew 6:33 "But seek ye first the kingdom of God, and his righteousness; and all these things shall be added unto you."

Isaiah 55:3 "Incline your ear, and come unto me: hear, and your soul shall live; and I will make an everlasting covenant with you, even the sure mercies of David."

Biblical Foundation For Spiritual Growth & Maturity

Made in the USA
Columbia, SC
06 January 2025